Windows on the Cross

Windows on the Cross

TOM SMAIL

COWLEY PUBLICATIONS
Cambridge ✦ Boston
Massachusetts

Published in the United States of America by Cowley
Publications, a division of the Society of St. John the
Evangelist. No portion of this book may be reproduced, stored
in or introduced into a retrieval system, or transmitted, in any
form or by any means – including photocopying – without the
prior written permission of Cowley Publications,
except in the case of brief quotations embodied in
critical articles and reviews.

Library of Congress Cataloging-in-Publication Data can be
obtained from the Library of Congress, Washington, D.C.
or from Cowley Publications.

ISBN: 1–56101–123–1

The Scripture quotations in this publication are taken from
The New International Version, published and copyright 1973,
1978, and 1984 by the International Bible Society.

Phototypeset by Intype, London.
Printed and bound in Great Britain
by Redwood Books, Trowbridge.

Cowley Publications
28 Temple Place
Boston, Massachusetts 02111

For All Saints', Sanderstead,
with gratitude and affection.

Cowley Publications
is a ministry of the Society of St. John the
Evangelist, a religious community for men in the
Episcopal Church. Emerging from the Society's
tradition of prayer, theological reflection, and
diversity of mission, the press is centered in the rich
heritage of the Anglican Communion.

Cowley Publications seeks to provide books,
audio cassettes, and other resources for the ongoing
theological exploration and spiritual development
of the Episcopal Church and others in the body of
Christ. To this end, it is dedicated to developing a
new generation of theological writers, encouraging
them to produce timely, creative, and stimulating
publications of excellence, and making these
publications available widely, reaching both
clergy and lay persons.

Contents

Contents

Preface

This is the first book I have written that has not had the person and work of the Holy Spirit as its central theme. That, I trust, does not mean that the insights and inspiration of the Spirit are absent from its pages, because it would be a hopeless enterprise to write about the cross of Christ without relying totally upon the help of the Spirit of Christ.

Nevertheless the change of focus is significant, because I have come to realise again with fresh conviction that the renewing heart of the Christian message is not what happened at Pentecost but what happened at Calvary. The gifts and power of Pentecost are indeed God's precious and greatly needed gifts to his people, but they cannot be received or used aright unless we see that they are the gifts and the power won for us by the crucified Jesus and take their meaning and their character solely from him. The heart of renewal of which the Church in all its branches stands greatly in need today is not merely a renewal of pentecostal power and charismatic gifts, but, before and above all, a renewal of our relationship to God, of our release from sin and our participation in the self-giving love of Jesus. To give us these the Spirit has to lead us back to the cross.

These chapters are offered in the hope that they may help a little to open, for our understanding and for our praying, that road that leads to Calvary. This is not a technical theological work, but I hope that its readers will be able to see that it has a firm theological foundation. I have tried both to do justice to a many-sided and complex theme and at the same time to make it as accessible as possible to all those who are ready to engage with it. I have given special attention to the cross as God's saving act accomplished once and for all by Christ alone on our behalf, because this is the aspect of the matter that people nowadays find hardest to understand and is yet quite central to the good news that we need to hear and receive.

The chapters are quite short which, on the one hand, means that the treatment of the various themes is inevitably incomplete and even sketchy, but, on the other hand, leaves room for readers to fill in the outlines I offer with further study and meditation of their own. To help with this I have included at the end of each chapter some Points to Ponder which could be used either by individual readers or in study groups, perhaps with reference to the many biblical texts that are quoted throughout. These quotations are mainly from the New International Version, occasionally from the Jerusalem Bible and once or twice are translations of my own.

The book is dedicated with much gratitude and affection to my last parish, All Saints' in Sanderstead, in whose pulpit I first presented, albeit in different form, many of the ideas that appear here. I have also to thank Mary Duncan, a Reader in that parish, for her careful reading of the manuscript and my wife Truda for comments and corrections along the way.

TOM SMAIL
London, Epiphany 1995

1

Opening the Shutters

'When I survey the wondrous cross' – so Isaac Watts wrote in the hymn we all know. The verb he chose is worth thinking about; not, 'When I behold' or 'When I regard' but 'When I *survey*'. It is his way of telling us that the cross of Christ is so gloriously stupendous in its significance that it fills and dominates the whole Christian landscape. Like an architect faced with a skyscraper we can only set up the theodolites of faith at its foot and try as best we can to come to take the measure of what it means for ourselves and the world.

Martin Luther made the same point in a slightly different way when he said *Crux probat omnia* – everything is put to the test of the cross. You will know if your God is the authentic Christian God if he has the kind of love which, at the climax of his purposes for his world, could give his Son to die for us on the cross. You will know if your estimate of the human plight is adequate if you realise that the only way out of it is not anything we could do for ourselves or by ourselves, but only in what Jesus did for us on Calvary. For Christians you can only begin to take account of the breadth, depth, length and height of God's love when you realise that 'God demonstrates his own love for us in this: While we were still sinners, Christ died for us' (Romans 5:8). For Christians the only goodness that counts ultimately is not moral respectability or dutiful conformity to divine commandments but that

1

there should be reflected in us something of that generous self-giving love that Jesus, himself the perfect reflection of his Father's nature, showed to people who had proved themselves to be quite unworthy of it. *Crux probat omnia* – Christian authenticity in all these realms depends how in them all we relate to the cross.

We are living through a time of great perplexity for most Christians. The society we have known shows many frightening signs of disintegrating all around us. Institutions that once were unmoving landmarks of stability – the monarchy, parliament, the police, the judiciary and the Church itself – have come under intense scrutiny and attack and deeply disturbing weaknesses have been exposed. News of wars, famine, human cruelty and injustice pour in upon us from every side. The advance of science has forced on us new moral dilemmas that we do not know how to tackle and resolve, and these have often to be faced not just in theory or in general but affect the lives of many families and reach down into the most intimate, sensitive areas of our own lives, leaving us confused and looking for help.

That is why I invite you to 'survey the wondrous cross', not to find instant answers to particular questions but so that we can find our bearings and our confidence again in the way that God deals with the confusion and destructiveness of his world and to discover in that some clues about how we in our turn might respond to and deal with the situations that personally and socially we have to face.

We can start by using our imaginations. Think for a moment of a very large house arranged round the four sides of a large internal courtyard in the middle of which stands a huge cross. This is not a country house set in tranquil parkland; it is surrounded by all the rush and squalor of a great city. Every door gives straight on to a pavement and there is an entrance from the street to the central courtyard on every side; the way from the world to the cross and from the cross to the world stands open, but is not much used.

On all the four wings of the house that surround the courtyard there are windows. The outside windows that overlook the street are clean and uncurtained so that there is a good view of the world and the inhabitants of the house are well aware of what is going on outside and can often be seen at the windows looking out with sad looks and perplexed eyes.

The inside windows that look out on the cross are far less used. They have not been cleaned and polished with any regularity so that they are dirty and some of them are even shuttered, so that no light has been able to come through them for a long time, with the result that the family in the house that is so well informed and so cast down by what is going on in the world around it knows far less about the cross that stands at the centre of its own grounds. It cannot tell the world about the cross or invite the world to the cross because it understands so little about it and its great need is to unshutter and polish the windows through which that cross could again come into view.

Some of these windows are very old, they might even be called ancient lights and the glass in them is not as transparent as it once was, so that it takes some care to discern what lies beyond it. But in one wing of the house there are new windows that have been constructed much later because it was thought that they gave a better view of the cross at the centre than the old ones could now offer. In fact, to see the cross from every side you have to look at it from all sorts of different angles, you have to walk round the whole house and look at it in every aspect through every window, the old as well as the new. The new windows will show you one side of it, but to avoid

3

one-sidedness you have to unshutter and polish up the old windows as well and take the trouble to look through the ancient glass so that you may see what can be seen only from there.

It is when you have unshuttered and looked through all these windows and let the radiance from the cross shine in through them that you will be able to look again at the world and see it differently and afresh in the light that streams from the cross, and perhaps even to persuade some passers-by to make use of the access through the house from the street to the cross.

This little parable is not too hard to unravel; the house at the heart of the city is the Church of Jesus Christ that looks out on the one side on the surrounding world and on the other on the cross where God took the decisive step for the rescuing of that world from its confusion and misery. Through the Church the cross is to have access to the streets and the person in the street is to have access to the cross. If however that is to happen the Church itself has to keep on surveying that cross or, in terms of our parable, it has to look through all the windows that have been provided so that it may see the different aspects of all that God has done in Christ. The ancient lights that are hard to see through and so often remain shuttered and unused are the ways in which the writers of the New Testament look at the cross, and the new windows are the different ways in which some Christian teachers have tried to understand it today.

The Jewish temple, the Greek slave market and the Roman law court are institutions that belong to worlds that are far removed from the one that we live in today but that were everyday realities to the people for whom the New Testament authors were writing. It is therefore understandable that when they are trying to get over to people the mysterious reality of what God was doing

4

when Jesus died on the cross they should speak in terms of the temple, the market and the law court that people knew.

So, it is to the worship of the temple that Jews knew well that they turn when they describe Jesus as the Lamb of God who takes away the sins of the world or as the great High Priest who offers himself to God in atoning sacrifice on behalf of all his people. In the same way when they speak of the cross as a great act of redemption, their ideas come from the markets where slaves were set free from the masters who formerly owned them when the appropriate price had been paid. Again Paul especially speaks the language of the law courts when he says that we were justified by what Jesus did for us in his death and resurrection. On him, on behalf of all of us, God's just sentence of death was executed, by him God's righteous demands upon us were fully met, so that in relation to him we are acquitted, and made acceptable to God, the righteous Judge of all the earth.

For us to read that last paragraph feels like being removed from the everyday world with its familiar ideas and language into a special biblical and theological realm with all its specialised jargon that most people have not been trained to understand and are reluctant to cope with. All of this only goes to show how shuttered and obscure the main New Testament windows on the cross are even for Christian people in our day, let alone the outside world that needs to hear its message.

The result is that when we ask ourselves or when we are asked by others why the cross is so central to the Christian gospel, without the biblical insights that would enable us to give a convincing answer, we are left saying vague things like, 'Because it shows how much God loves us and that we should follow Jesus' example by loving one another in the same way.' That is no doubt very true,

5

but it leaves quite unanswered why God should have thought it necessary to prove his love in this particular and quite peculiar way by sending his Son to die an agonising and humiliating death on a Roman gallows.

To help us understand all that, the New Testament windows on Calvary are indispensable and in fact far less impenetrable than they might at first seem. If we will take the trouble, using as much expert help as we need, to take down the shutters and polish the panes, we shall discover that the ancient lights are still up to their original job and will bring us into the bright and warm beams of God's grace that flow out from the cross to illuminate our minds, warm our hearts and give us a unique and specific piece of good news to pass on to other people that is just not available anywhere else at all.

In other words, behind the difficult and uncongenial ideas and images that come from the customs and rituals of temple, market and court at a particular time in human history, there is hidden a proclamation of what Jesus was about on Calvary that is relevant, releasing and life-giving for people at every period and in every society, and we have to be ready to look again at what the New Testament writers are saying, so that message may be relevantly heard and faithfully relayed in our own day. That is what we shall be trying to do in the chapters that follow, both to inform our minds but still more to stimulate a response of believing gratitude deep within us towards the crucified and risen Lord.

So we must unshutter the old windows, but we must also go to the modern wing of the building and look through the new windows and see what we can learn from our more contemporary perspectives on the cross. If the biblical writers found in their environment ways of speaking about the death of Jesus that communicated to those who belonged to their world in their day, we need to see if we can do the same in our world and our day. These more modern approaches will not be biblical in the sense that they use the language and ideas of the biblical writers, but it may be that they say in different language and ideas the same thing that the Bible is saying or even make explicit aspects of the cross that are only implicit in the scriptural record.

We shall be looking at two of these more modern windows on the cross. People in our own day have found it helpful to think of Calvary as the decisive battle in which Jesus takes on the forces of sin, death, hell and the devil in all their ferocity and defeats them on our behalf. That way of thinking has, as we shall see, its origins in the Bible and is developed by some of the Fathers of the Church, but it has had a special appeal in the twentieth century ever since it was promoted by the Swedish theologian, Gustaf Aulén, in his very influential book *Christus Victor* – Christ the Conqueror, which appeared in 1931 and has been in print ever since.

More recently and in reaction to the horrors of the twentieth century and in particular to the Jewish Holocaust, theologians like the German Jürgen Moltmann have invited us to see the cross, not so much as the place where God in Christ atones for our sins, but rather the place where he shares our sufferings and our death and by sharing them makes for us a way through them to resurrection and new life. Many have looked through that window in our day and seen the cross with new eyes and we need to ask what that approach is saying to us and how it relates to the more obviously biblical approaches. How does what we see through this new window relate to what we see through the ancient lights?

To ease ourselves into that programme we shall in the next chapter start by looking through a window that is situated at the point in the building where the old and

7

the new are joined together. Our first approach to the cross will be one that is both biblical and contemporary, because it speaks of Calvary as an act of reconciliation in which God takes the initiative in restoring the broken relationships between himself and his people. Quarrels and reconciliations, the breaking and remaking of relationships, are such fundamental and universal human concerns that they are of immediate relevance to every one whether we live in the first century or the twentieth, and we all prick up our ears and want to know more when we hear Paul saying, 'God was reconciling the world to himself in Christ . . . And he has committed to us the message of reconciliation' (2 Corinthians 5:19).

Before however we can get on with our task, there is one important and often made objection that we need to listen to and, if we can, answer. It goes something like this. Does this whole matter really need to be so complicated? We agree with what you have just been saying about the vital importance of a restoration of right relationships between us and God, but we do not see why that need involve the suffering and death of Jesus on the cross. Perhaps what we need to do is not unshutter all these obscure windows that you have been talking about and instead unlock and open the door marked repentance so that we can find on the other side the God who is waiting and ready freely to forgive us without the offering of any sacrifice, the paying of any price, the suffering of any death sentence. Human repentance will always find divine forgiveness without any cross standing in between. Isn't this something that Jews, Muslims and Christians can agree about provided Christians will abandon the views of atonement that make God's pardon depend on the death of Jesus that the other religions find both grotesque and unnecessary?

Furthermore, our objector might continue, isn't the simple correlation of repentance and forgiveness as the

8

means to reconciliation in line with the teaching of Jesus himself, before it was needlessly complicated and confused by Paul and the other New Testament writers? In the parable of the prodigal son, for example, when the son comes to himself and returns to the father, he finds waiting for him the forgiveness and the welcome that he had not dared to hope for and the sins of yesterday are wiped out not by an atoning death but by the gracious generosity of his father's love and the only sacrifice around is that of the fatted calf? If you are looking for a gospel that is easy to understand by people who are not experts in first-century religion, why look any further than the message of this parable? Whatever you have done, however far you have wandered, whatever disgrace you have brought upon yourself, come back to God and you can be sure that he will forgive you and restore you to full membership of his family and rejoice over you with a longing Father's love.

To give a full answer to that objection we shall need all the following chapters, because in them we shall be trying to show in many different ways how the message of the cross is in fact at the very heart of the gospel and its message is not credible, complete or effective without it. We can however end this chapter with a preliminary answer that will be filled out by all that follows.

Like many objections the one we have just outlined is right in what it affirms but wrong in what it denies. The parable of the prodigal son draws our attention to two factors that are indeed at the very heart of the gospel, God's unconditional willingness to forgive and our need to come back to him, to confess where we have been wrong and to enter into the welcoming reality of that forgiveness; to do that very personally and specifically is a central part of the Lenten discipline to which we submit ourselves, and nothing that we go on to say must be

9

allowed to contradict or in any way lessen the importance of these two points.

Nevertheless, the parable cannot be read in and for itself, it rings true only when we remember who it was that told it and realise that his whole story gives this story a depth, a completeness and a credibility that it does not have in itself. As Helmut Thielicke puts it

> Jesus, who tells this parable, is pointing to himself, between the lines and back of every word. If this were just anyone telling us this story of a good and kindly Father we could only laugh. We could only say, 'How do you know there's a God who seeks me, who takes any interest in my lostness, who, indeed, suffers because of me? Why do you tell such nursery tales?'*

The parable however proves itself to be no nursery tale when it is told by Jesus whose heavenly Father does much more than wait longingly for his lost children to return, but who in his own words has come in his Father's name 'to seek and to save what was lost' (Luke 19:10) and in so doing 'to give his life as a ransom for many' (Matthew 20:28) as the cost of that seeking. The father of the parable becomes a credible figure when, from the story of Jesus, we see that he is the God who 'so loved the world that he gave his one and only Son, that whoever believes in him shall not perish but have eternal life' (John 3:16). The God of the gospel is even more gracious than the God of the parable; he does not just wait and long for us to come back to him, he sends his Son who is one with himself to the far country of Calvary to do what needs to be done to bring us home. The parable points to the cross because it is told by a Christ who is on his way to the cross.

Furthermore the parable speaks about God's uncon-

---

* *The Waiting Father* (London, James Clarke, 1986), p. 28.

ditional readiness to forgive us all that has gone wrong in the past that has spoilt and broken our relationship with him. But complete reconciliation is about more than forgiveness of the past. If I am to live in harmony with someone with whom I have quarrelled, we need not only to forgive each other and accept each other, we need to agree with each other, to make sure that the old cycle will not repeat itself and we will fall out all over again. As the prophet Amos asked long ago, 'Can two walk together unless they are agreed?' (Amos 3:3).

If I am to be reconciled to God, it will not do to live in a miserable alternation of sinning and being forgiven again and again and again, as many of us know from bitter experience. Being graciously and generously pardoned we need also to be radically and completely changed, so that we become of one mind, will, character and purpose with God. Otherwise the son who rebelled against life in his father's house before he departed will be liable to rebel again, to say nothing of his elder brother who at the end of the parable shows himself to be completely out of tune with his father, although he has never departed at all.

That is a side of things that the parable does not deal with, but as we shall see it is right at the heart of what Jesus is dealing with on the cross where he takes our rebellious humanity down to a well deserved death and replaces it with a new humanity that is totally in tune with God.

As Geoffrey Paul puts it,

... When sin has really got its grip on a situation, offers of forgiveness and individual attempts to do better are in the end insufficient, ineffective and marginal in their effects. Some sort of death is the only way in which the canker in the whole system can be attacked and overcome. Repentance and forgiveness do not deliver

11

the individual penitent *from the situation*, do not strike at the root of his predicament. Only a total remedy affecting the situation as a whole can offer the individual any real hope of a new start.[†]

That total remedy that affects the situation as a whole is what Christians have always found at the cross. There we see how God's will to forgive, so powerfully pictured in the parable, is worked out in the sending of his Son to seek and save us, which involves not only his accepting of us as we are, but his remaking of us, in a way that reflects both his holiness and his love, into what he has always wanted us to be.

What that means we shall see more clearly as we proceed, but there can be no sight of it without looking to what was done on Calvary; if the light of God's grace is indeed to shine fully upon us, we must unshutter all the windows and survey the wondrous cross.

POINTS TO PONDER

- Through what window have you been surveying the cross up till now? How would you answer the question, Why did Jesus have to die?

- 'The renewing heart of the Christian message is not what happened at Pentecost but what happened at Calvary.' Do you agree?

- Think further about Geoffrey Paul's statement, 'Repentance and forgiveness do not deliver the individual penitent from the situation, do not strike at the root of his predicament.'

† *A Pattern of Faith* (London, Churchman Publishing, 1986), p. 61.

2

Reconciliation

It is, I think, Bishop Lesslie Newbigin who tells of a visit to the Christian community in one of the villages of his former diocese in South India. The communion service he was leading for them proceeded normally until they reached the point where the members of the congregation were to exchange the Peace with one another. When he invited them to do so, the liturgical action was rudely interrupted by protesting voices and fingers pointing to two men standing as far away as possible from each other. 'There is no peace here', people said, 'because these two men have quarrelled over the boundaries of their fields and are going to law against each other. There will be no peace among us till they are reconciled.'

Whereupon the whole congregation left the church and went to the disputed boundaries, and, under the guidance of its leaders, heard the claims of the two antagonists, adjudicated a just settlement and a personal reconciliation between them, and only then returned to the church to share the Peace and the communion that followed with a reality and joy that can only come when the issues that divide people and lead to bad feeling between them have been honestly faced and effectively dealt with.

At a service like that reality breaks into ritual with a vengeance; Sunday worship and the concerns of everyday life suddenly come into alarmingly close contact with each other, in precisely the way Jesus intended when he said,

'Therefore, if you are offering your gift at the altar and there remember that your brother has something against you, leave your gift there in front of the altar. First go and be reconciled to your brother; then come and offer your gift. Settle matters quickly with your adversary who is taking you to court' (Matthew 5:23–5).

That little Indian congregation took these words seriously and literally in a way that puts most of us to shame. No doubt that service took a long time, but we might ask ourselves how long a communion service would last in the congregations to which we belong, if, before we took communion, we had to sort out all the quarrels that secretly put' the members of our churches at odds with one another and, as long as they are unresolved, inject their hidden poison into our worship and life that can suppurate and break surface and cause trouble at any moment in all kinds of unexpected ways. Peace in our relationships depends on the action we take to remove the causes of division; forgiveness becomes real only when something happens that radically changes the attitude of the hostile parties to each other and, as far as possible, puts right the wrongs that have been inflicted and suffered by them.

The New Testament, not least the Lord's Prayer itself, teaches that forgiveness on the horizontal level between two people stands in the closest connection with God's forgiveness of all of us on the vertical level, so that the basic principles that apply to one apply to the other also. If in both cases forgiveness is to lead to full reconciliation, then the issues that separate the parties have to be faced and resolved. To quote Amos again, 'Can two walk together unless they are agreed?' (Amos 3:3).

Bearing all this in mind we can look now at two passages in the writings of Paul in which he speaks explicitly of the work of Christ on the cross in terms of reconcili-

14

ation between God and human beings. The first is in Romans 5:10: 'When we were God's enemies, we were reconciled to him through the death of his Son'. God's enemies – that phrase throws us back on our heels when we hear it and many of us will instinctively want to protest against it. Sure, we make our mistakes and occasionally do things that we should not do, but basically we are well-intentioned people whose aim in life is to do as much good as we can and to write us off indiscriminately as God's enemies is to perpetrate an undeserved slander against us.

One of the things that makes it very hard for us to appreciate what the New Testament writers want to tell us about the death of Jesus on the cross is, to put it starkly, that they were worried about their sins and we are not. For them the starting-point for talking about reconciliation was that the way we live and the kind of people that we constantly show ourselves to be make such a rift between us and God that it takes nothing less than the death of God's Son to bring us together again. We were his enemies and it took what happened on Calvary to make us his friends.

We live in a society where none of that makes sense any more and the refusal to be serious about sin or to believe that God could take sins seriously has spread from the world to the Church. In a recent article Professor Mary Gray asks, 'Is sinfulness still an accepted category in our society for either the religious believer or non-believer?' and she goes on to report that when the University of Louvain in Belgium 'surveyed the attitudes on sin and guilt of European Christians in 1985, 40 per cent of those interviewed *admitted that they had never experienced any feelings of regret about their actions.*'*

* In *Scottish Journal of Theology* (1994), vol. 47, no. 2, p. 223.

No doubt there is a certain amount of defiant bravado in such a response; it is hard to believe that the Christian conscience is quite as quiescent as that. If it were, the gospel and especially the gospel of the cross would have little to say to such people. On the word of Jesus, 'It is not the healthy who need a doctor, but the sick. I have not come to call the righteous but sinners to repentance' (Luke 5:31–2). Of course there is irony in that remark, because the diagnosis of Jesus was that the sickness of sin was most deadly in those who refused to admit that they were suffering from it. We need to heed his warning that, if we claim that we are all right as we are, we are in danger of cutting ourselves off from his ministry and putting ourselves outside the range of his grace. For such people all talk of reconciliation is irrelevant. If there is nothing wrong, there is nothing needing to be put to rights between us and God.

Most of us would not go anything like that far; we have sufficient self-knowledge and our conscience is active enough to tell us that we are *not* all right as we are, that there are things we have done and not done, outward actions and inner attitudes of which we have good reason to be ashamed. But for most of the time we do not let any of that worry us too much and we very quickly console ourselves that God is so understanding and compassionate in his judgements of us and so generous in his readiness to forgive that if we tell him about it, he will pardon it and it need trouble neither him nor us any more.

Such an attitude makes it hard to come to terms with the cross; perhaps that is one reason why so many of the windows through which our forebears looked at it are shuttered and unused, why the biblical presumption that 'Christ died for our sins' has failed to make much impact upon us and why in particular the statement that we are God's enemies needing to be reconciled to him by the

16

death of his Son seems to us to be exaggerated and extreme.

If that is indeed how we feel, we need all the more to look at the cross so that what happens there can show us the dangerous depth and deadly nature of our conflict with God and how much that conflict needs to be resolved. That is indeed what his own encounter with the risen Jesus revealed to Paul. On the road to Damascus he was shown not just the answer to his problem but what his problem really was. When he started out on that journey he was, as he tells us in Philippians 4, congratulating himself on his Jewish credentials and his life lived in meticulous observance of the strictest code of moral righteousness. If ever there was a friend of God it was Saul of Tarsus and the final proof of his zeal for the God of Israel was his relentless persecution of the heretical sect that had gathered round Jesus.

Then suddenly this very Jesus confronted him in all the majesty of his ascended glory to ask the question, 'Saul, Saul, why are you persecuting me?' and in a moment his whole perception of his relationship to God is radically overthrown. He saw himself as God's friend but now, in the living presence of the Crucified, it dawned upon him that all the time he has really been God's persecutor, God's enemy. When Paul uses that phrase in Romans, no doubt his own experience is not far in the background.

So with ourselves, left to our own estimation of ourselves, we can easily be complacent about ourselves and about God's attitude towards us when we go wrong, but if we look through the windows at the cross, if we renew our relationship with the Jesus who once died on the cross, we see in his light both what we have done and what we have failed to do, we see that we are much more like the crucifiers than the crucified.

'Were you there when they crucified my Lord?' In the

deserting cowardice that ran away from what it had promised to follow, in the dishonest manoeuvring of the priests who were terrified of the upheaval that exposure to Jesus would require of their church and of themselves, in the self-interest of Pilate who knew Jesus was innocent but was not prepared to risk his job in standing up for him, in the crowd who shouted what everybody else was shouting without looking at the issues involved, in the soldiers who mocked and kicked a good man when he was down – in all these I was there. When we can get our hands on God, this is what we do to him. When the divine love that we see in Jesus comes among us, not only do we fail to imitate it, we turn upon it; not only are we not like him, but all the priorities by which we live turn us against him.

The people who crucified Jesus were not monsters of iniquity, they were people exactly like ourselves who meant well, but did badly, who had high standards but fell short of them far more fatally than they knew, who partly through their personal fault and partly because they were shaped by the fallen world in which they lived showed themselves to be enemies of God. 'He died for our sins' exposes his grace but it also exposes our disgrace. Because of people like us, he was rejected and crucified, and by people like us the love that died on Calvary is still rejected today. When we are looking through the window at the cross, it does not perhaps sound quite so far-fetched to call us 'enemies of God'.

And not perhaps so far-fetched either to speak, as Paul does in the same context of Romans 5, of God's wrath against his enemies, a wrath that is not irrational rage but the natural reaction of love against all that defies and rejects love. The love of God and the wrath of God are not two contradictory qualities within the life of God, as if he loved us sometimes but was angry with us at others and you could never quite foretell how he was going to be. Wrath is love reacting against the self-centredness, the violence, hatred and destructiveness that are incompatible with love. A God who patted us on the head whatever we did and said, 'There, there, it is all right, I forgive you,' would be a God who did not take his own love seriously, just as over-indulgent parents who let their children off with anything are not showing love but are failing to love.

As every good parent knows, love makes you angry with your children when they show themselves to be unloving and so in danger of not being the people that they were intended to be. When they start keeping company, adopting priorities, pursuing courses of action that defy everything that makes life good and that are potentially destructive for themselves and for others, then if we love them, our love has to be tough enough to say no to what they are doing and becoming. That is a pointer to the Father's love that says no to us when we give vent to the selfishness, violence and injustice by which we crucified his Son.

In order to be true to itself, love has to be tough and love has to be angry, but that can never be the last word; precisely in order to be true to itself love can never finally break off the relationship with those with whom it has good reason to be angry, it will always be looking for an opportunity for reconciliation and it will always be ready to do whatever needs to be done to bring that reconciliation about.

As in all quarrels the initiative for reconciliation will always come from one side, not necessarily from the party that has caused the quarrel but often from the party that has most love. That, according to Paul is what has happened in order to bring about the healing of our broken relationship with God. 'When we were God's enemies, we were reconciled to him through the death of his Son' (Romans 5:10). God did not retire into hurt aloofness and wait for us to make overtures of repentance towards him, his attitude to us is not, 'When they say they are sorry, then I might think about forgiving them.' His love proves itself to be far more gloriously generous than that. As Paul puts it a few verses earlier in the same chapter, 'God demonstrates his own love for us in this: While we were still sinners, Christ died for us' (Romans 5:8). On the very Calvary where we erect a cross and sharpen nails with which to crucify him, God in his love is taking the initiative that will heal the breach and bring himself and us back together again.

Paul spells that out in greater detail in the second passage in which he speaks of the cross in terms of reconciliation, namely 2 Corinthians 5:18–21. The key verses are 18 and 19, 'All this is from God, who reconciled us to himself through Christ and gave us the ministry of reconciliation: that God was reconciling the world to himself in Christ, not counting men's sins against them. And he has committed to us the message of reconciliation.' The initiative is God's, it is God who pays the cost of it, our part is simply to respond to what he has done for us and to make it known to the whole world on whose behalf it was done. The passage we have just been quoting continues, 'We are therefore Christ's ambassadors, as though God were making his appeal through us. We implore you on Christ's behalf: Be reconciled to God' (v. 20). He has done it all, your job is to accept and receive what he has done and on his behalf to make it known to everybody else as well.

The uniqueness of the Christian good news lies hidden in these verses. I remember talking to a perplexed theological student who in the course of her studies of other religions had rightly been impressed and indeed rebuked by a video she had seen about a Sikh holy man who obviously had a spirituality and a prayerfulness that put most Christians to shame. Her very understandable reaction was to ask what she could possibly have to say to a man like that who had a serious commitment to the search for God that made her theological study look superficial by comparison.

She had in fact much to offer him; although she could not outdo his piety she could tell him about what can only be learned from Jesus and supremely at his cross, that the God whom all the religions in their different ways seek does not wait for us to find him by our deep thinking, our good living, our prayers or our piety, but has taken the initiative by coming himself in his Son – 'God was in Christ' – into a world that crucified him in order to bring us back to himself.

Many of the religions know about a God who will receive us, forgive us and accept us when we have put our lives in good moral order and become faithful and dedicated in our prayers and religious practices, but it is in Old Testament Israel and supremely in his Son Jesus Christ that we must look to find that God is ready to do far more than receive us when we make ourselves acceptable to him, but actually comes to seek and to save that which was lost. He loves not just his friends who obey him but his enemies who defy him and takes the hard road to Bethlehem and to Calvary for love of those who, for all their fine religion, in the last resort had no place for him but a cross. We owe it to Sikhs and to the followers of all the other religions, not because we despise them but because we respect them, to be the ambassadors of the God that has done for us far beyond anything we could have deserved or imagined, to let them see him in Jesus coming to bring our world back into his friendship and peace.

We need to emphasise that God's love is *tough* love, tough enough certainly not only to refuse to compromise with a humanity that had made itself his enemies by refusing to receive or to live out of that love, but, most gloriously tough enough for Calvary, tough enough to go the whole distance at tremendous cost to make these very enemies his friends.

Equally we need to emphasise that this tough love is *God*'s love. Christians have sometimes got this wrong and spoken as if on the cross a loving Jesus had died to persuade an angry God to forgive us and accept us. There is not a trace of anything like this in the whole New Testament. In our 2 Corinthians passage Jesus dies *not* to reconcile God to us but to reconcile us to God; God's will to forgive and receive us is not the *result* of Calvary; it is what motivates the Father to send us his Son to do at tremendous cost what needs to be done to bring us back to him. 'God so loved the world that he gave his only Son' (John 3:16). The love of Jesus does not procure the love of God, it *is* the eternal love of God come to earth for us.

That love works by making contact again – that is where reconciliation always has to start. When people who have fallen out never meet, attitudes begin to harden, anger curdles into bitterness, our memories of each other become distorted and unreal and the only hope of a breakthrough is for the parties to meet either by chance or by arrangement. To arrange such a meeting is always a risky strategy, because the result could be that new insult is added to old injury and the quarrel is worsened rather than resolved, but it is a risk that has to be taken, because without contact there will be no possibility of peace.

In the coming of Jesus God arranges to meet those who have made themselves his enemies and to meet them as one of them on their own ground – the Son of God becomes man and in his words and his works gives evidence of his Father's willingness to love his enemies, to heal those whose lives in different ways have been broken by their living in a world that has cut itself off from its source of life in God.

The risk is that God's loving initiative will be rejected, that his coming instead of renewing the relationship will finally end it, and when God's love is crucified on Calvary, it looks as if that is exactly what has happened. God is not just disregarded and disobeyed, he is done to death on the cross.

Yet here is the marvel of it, that the death of Jesus which seems to range God and humanity in irreconcilable opposition is the very means by which they can be reunited. The words of Jesus from the cross point clearly in that direction, 'Father, forgive them, for they do not know what they are doing' and to the criminal beside him, 'Today, you will be with me in paradise.'

That is the mystery that Paul is pondering in the final verse of 2 Corinthians 5, 'God made him [Jesus] who had no sin to be sin for us, so that in him we might become the righteousness of God' (v. 21). Jesus on the cross penetrated in love right into the heart of the mess that we had made, he took on himself the hatred, the violence, the self-concern, the cowardice that had constructed his cross and that were the consequences of our attitudes and actions not of his own. He took them and he transformed them. He took the dire and deadly outworking of our sin on to himself where it encountered his love, he took the cross which was the result of human wrongdoing and made it a place where he did what was right in offering himself to God on our behalf.

Here is a man who is totally like us, who has experienced the worst that people could do to him, who has felt the hatred but never yielded to it, who has suffered the pain but not been broken by it, who has been the victim

23

of violence but has not retaliated with violent reactions of his own; here is the man who has remained God's friend when everybody around him was proving to be God's enemy. Here is the man who is in right relationship with God when everybody else is in wrong relationship with God. When God looks at the cross where his enemies have done their worst he sees this man who on that very cross has proved himself God's friend, on whose dying love he delights because it is a reflection of his own. Here his own love is mirrored back to him out of the darkness of sin and death; this man who prays for God's enemies is himself God's friend and that forgiving renewing friendship stretches out from this man to all who trust him and identify themselves with him.

All this is offered to us as a promise that what happened on Calvary can also through Jesus happen to us. In ourselves we have all kinds of things that stand between us and God, that tell us that he is not pleased with us as we are and that we are not at peace with him. The good news is that Jesus has come into our situation and taken on all these things that divide us from God and swamped them with his love. He has done it on Calvary for the whole world and, if we will bring our personal situation and ask him to cope with it, he will do the same for us.

On the cross God's love has reached down and dealt with human sin; the Man on the cross is the promise and the guarantee that even in the midst of a sinful world God and people can be friends again. Through Jesus that peace, that reconciliation, that friendship is available for us. That is what we can begin to see as we look through this window at the cross, and if we see it, it will require us to respond to it. 'All this is from God who reconciled us to himself through Christ . . . We implore you on Christ's behalf: Be reconciled to God.'

POINTS TO PONDER

- What do you make of Paul's description of us as God's enemies?

- In what way does God's forgiveness of us depend on our willingness to forgive others?

- Does the centrality of its message of reconciliation through the cross make the Christian gospel unique among all the religions?

we are like drunks on the street and in our midst is a man who sacrifices his safety, his quiet home, his peacefulness to come to us as a friend. He knows we are angry and don't want his help. He shows his love by staying in our midst and working to bring us back into our peaceful homes.

When we forgive and sacrifice for reconciliation we are acting like god in Christ. Through our own acting we can better understand god's love for us (the extreme nature of it) and thus understand how much he loves us.

3

Sacrifice

Our last window was domestic, our next is ecclesiastical. In thinking of the cross as reconciliation we were looking at it in the context of fractured and restored personal relationships, an area in which we are all deeply involved and interested but the next window is of a quite different shape. It is stained glass and Gothic, and through it we are invited to look at the cross in the context of the rituals of the Jewish temple and its services, which are both remote from anything in our own experience and in large measure repulsive to the modern sensibilities that we all share.

One of the professors under whom I studied Old Testament in Edinburgh used to take a delight in attacking young students of a more fundamentalist bent by confronting them with lurid pictures of ancient Hebrews bringing long strings of bullocks, sheep, lambs and birds to be offered in sacrifice by the priests in the temple. He would conjure up for us in graphic phrases the flash of priestly knives cutting animal throats, the flowing of red steaming blood, the smoke and stench of roasting meat as the sacrifice was burnt in the fire and would end up with the mocking comment, 'Nothing very spiritual about that!' That is a reaction that most of us would echo and share and indeed go on to ask what a performance of that kind could possibly have to tell us about the death of Jesus on the cross.

In spite of that, however, we need to recognise that the window of Old Testament sacrifice is one through which the New Testament writers insist on looking at Calvary and, although such an approach may be alien and uncongenial to us, we need to ask what it was that they saw through this window that made it so important for them and whether, if we have the patience to listen to what they say when they talk in these terms, we might see it too.

In the letter to the Hebrews Jesus on the cross is seen as both Priest and sacrifice. As the Old Testament priesthood offered many animal sacrifices to God to cleanse the people from sin and to make them holy, so 'unlike the other high priests, he [Jesus] does not need to offer sacrifices day after day . . . He sacrificed for their sins once for all when he offered himself' (Hebrews 7:27). The whole letter is an elaboration of that central statement.

Other New Testament writers tend to think of Jesus in connection with the sacrifice of the Passover lambs, whose blood marked the doors of the houses of God's people in Egypt, so that by that blood they were saved from the angel of death who passed over their houses. When the New Testament speaks of Jesus as the Lamb of God who takes away the sins of the world (John 1:29), or when it tells us as it often does that we are saved from our sins by the blood of Christ (1 Peter: 19), it is remembering the Passover feast and saying that what the sacrificial lamb's blood on the doors did for Israel in Egypt, helps us to understand what Jesus was doing for the whole world on the cross.

However, we are not Jews; the Passover festival, let alone the temple sacrifices that stopped when the Romans destroyed the temple in AD 70, are not things of which we have any experience or for which we have much sympathy. It may be however that there are things we do in

27

our culture that are expressing the same human needs and attitudes that the Jews expressed when they offered sacrifices and that can give us at least a clue as to what they were about, and therefore as to what the sacrifice of Jesus was also about.

In my last parish there was a flower shop with the strange name of Occasionally Yours and these two words express rather well both what we are saying to one another when we give flowers and what the Jews were saying to God when they offered their sacrifices. For there are special occasions when we want to identify with people and express our closeness to them, and one way of doing it is by a gift of flowers. It might be at a time of bereavement in order to convey our sympathy and fellow feeling with people in their loss, or it might be a time of a significant anniversary or a great success when we want to tell people that we are congratulating them and rejoicing with them. The flowers might convey our gratitude for what somebody has done for us, or they might be a peace offering by which we are expressing our sorrow for a wrong done or a hurt caused and asking to be forgiven and have our friendship restored. In all these situations we can 'say it with flowers' and they are more eloquent than our words because we have taken the trouble to go out and get them and have invested our money in them so that they represent a bit of ourselves, they say to people, 'On this special occasion, with this special gift I want to be yours.'

With their sacrifices the Jews of the Old Testament were saying much the same to God. In a completely different social system where your resources consisted not of your money but your livestock, people said it not with flowers but with birds and animals. Different sacrifices said different things; the thank offering expressed gratitude to God for his generosity, in the fellowship offering you identified yourself afresh with God's cause and laws and put yourself at his disposal and service. We are doing the same sort of thing when we lay our money on the altar in church on Sundays; we thank God for his goodness, we give something that is ours for his purposes in his world as a sign that we are putting what we have and what we are at his disposal.

Among all these sacrifices there was also the sin offering that was provided to deal with situations where something had gone wrong between God and his people. As the appointed way of putting things right again, as a sign of repentance and as a plea for forgiveness they came again to the altar and presented a sacrifice. On all these special occasions they were saying to God, 'In spontaneous gratitude, in costly commitment, in humble repentance, we are yours.'

It was not therefore surprising that when the New Testament writers were trying to make sense of what happened to Jesus when he died on the cross they should, as we have seen, have come to regard his death on Calvary as the ultimate sacrifice that fulfilled but also superseded all that had gone before.

The writer to the Hebrews in particular is disillusioned with the Old Testament sacrificial system. The very fact that the sin offerings have to be endlessly repeated is a sign that they do not work, because, in spite of them, people go on sinning and in any case killing animals cannot in itself change or transform our relationship with God. 'It is impossible', he says, 'for the blood of bulls and goats to take away sins' (Hebrews 10:4).

The ultimate sacrifice, that one that does deal relevantly with the sin problem and that does not have to be repeated because once it is made it goes on being effective for ever, is not anything that happens on the altar in the temple, it is what happens with Jesus on the cross. That

29

is the central conviction of the letter to the Hebrews, Christ 'has appeared once for all at the end of the ages to do away with sin by the sacrifice of himself' (9:26). The temple priests sacrificed animals, Jesus sacrificed himself; on Calvary the offerer and the offering, the gift and the giver are one. What this priest does he does only once, because he has done it so completely that it will never need to be done again. On this one occasion on behalf of us all he says to God, 'Now and for ever, I am yours.' That deals with sin because, in his saying that not just with his lips but with his life and in his death, sin is contradicted, repudiated and overcome.

To sin is to say to God in a thousand different ways, 'No, I am not yours. I will not live in thankful dependence upon you because I want to belong to myself. I will not commit myself to your will and your cause because my first commitment is to myself and my interests. I do not care very much about restoring and maintaining my relationship with you if that is going to interfere with my freedom to do what I want with my own life.' Jesus offers himself to his Father on the cross saying 'I did it your way', in utter contradiction to the favourite song of the sinner, 'I did it my way'.

Here on the cross is a man who does for all of us what none of us has been able to do for ourselves; he is the man who without holding back anything pours himself out in a great offering of self-giving to his Father and so inaugurates a new humanity that at last is restored to its right relationship of gratitude and commitment to the God who made us all. 'I am yours' – that is the signature tune of everything that Jesus is, says and does, so that everything he is, says and does is part of the sacrifice that is completed and consummated in his death on Calvary.

Hebrews expresses that by putting into his mouth the

30

words of Psalm 40, 'Sacrifices and offerings, burnt offerings and sin offerings you did not desire nor were you pleased with them. Then I said, "here I am, I have come to do your will, O God"' (10:5–7). Giving yourself to God so completely that in life and in death you do his will, that is the real offering, the ultimate sacrifice and Jesus has made it for us all.

Dr Trevor Hart of Aberdeen writes about the startling crucifix that stands outside the former parish church of St Paul's in Worcester, 'What is striking is the fact that the dying Christ, instead of hanging limply on the tree with head downcast, is gripping the cross, visibly embracing the death which it entails, and has his head thrust heavenwards, a look of triumph and doxological joy on his face.'*

That comment on that crucifix emphasises that when we look at the cross through the window of sacrifice, what we see is an action and not just a passion. Jesus is not just the victim helplessly enduring what others do to him, in his suffering he is intensely active, in an outgoing enthusiasm of self-giving love he is pouring out all that is in him to his Father on behalf of the world that they both love. In the terminology of Hebrews, he is the priest as well as the victim, the offerer as well as the offering.

When he says in Gethsemane, 'Not my will but yours be done' he is not submitting with helpless resignation to a horrible fate that he cannot avoid. On the contrary his dread of suffering, which is very real because he is very human, is overcome by his greater love for and trust in his Father, by his total identification with and availability for the saving purposes which he and his Father have for the world and which only his death on the cross can fulfil.

The old humanity symbolised by Adam tried to fulfil

* 'Atonement and Worship' in *Anvil* (1994), vol. 11, no. 3, pp. 210–11.

itself in proud independence of God and fell into all the troubles that beset us still; the new humanity inaugurated by Christ fulfils itself by giving everything to God on the cross and finding the life that leads on to Easter day. It is a good Lenten question to ask ourselves whether our own record and priorities show us to be children of Adam or brothers and sisters of Jesus. Are we busy with Adam saving our lives and so in danger of losing them, or are we with Jesus spending our lives in God's purposes and so receiving them back from him fresh and new?

We may however ask why the self-giving of Christ has to lead to the death of Christ. Was it not enough that all through his life in every possible way Jesus was expressing his loving obedience to his Father? Why does death need to come into it? The answer is that death is for all of us the ultimate point of trusting. We can control many things but not when and where and how we shall die. Therefore death is either the point of our final despairing or our ultimate trusting, the point at which everything else that we might trust is taken from us so that either we have nothing to trust and hope for or we go into the uncontrollable mystery trusting and hoping in God. The way we have lived, the kind of people we really are under all the disguises and masks that we wear often comes to its ultimate expression in the way that we die. Death, as Charles Wesley puts it, makes the sacrifice complete. It made Jesus' sacrifice complete; his whole life is summed up in his last words as Luke records them, 'Father, into your hands I commend my spirit' (Luke 23:46).

Even so, we can still ask why it had to be the kind of death that it was, the cruel and horrible agony of public crucifixion. The answer to that question brings us right to the heart of the matter. It had to be that kind of death because only that kind of death could deal with our sins. Hebrews says that without really explaining it; 'Without

32

the shedding of blood there is no forgiveness' (Hebrews 9:21) but the same letter points us in the right direction when the writer tells us that 'the blood of Christ, who through the eternal Spirit offered himself unblemished to God, [will] cleanse our consciences from acts that lead to death, so that we may serve the living God' (9:14).

The blood of Jesus, which in the New Testament always means his life poured out in death, has a cleansing quality about it. In suffering and dying he gets into the middle of the human situation of violence, pain and wrongdoing with its consequent pain and destruction, which has no future, because it is closed to God and shut off from the life that comes from him. But by sharing the consequences of sin on Calvary, by identifying himself with the suffering and the death that sin involves, he opens up that closed situation to God again so that it can be cleansed and made new. His self-giving love that opens up the human mess to the love of God that can heal it, is the means by which everything in our humanity that rebels against God can be washed away.

But washing powder, however powerfully detergent, is no use until it gets into the closest possible contact with the soiled and dirty clothes that it must wash. So with Jesus the spotless holiness of his totally God-centred life has to get into contact with all the God-defying things in us that it wants to wash away. Jesus' commitment to God becomes effective for other people only when it is made in the place where our sinful rebellious self-will reaches its climax.

Calvary is erected by the hands of priests who are unfaithful to their vocation, by Pilate whose job is to administer justice but who connives in a great injustice, by cruel soldiers, faithless disciples and a bloodthirsty crowd. It is human sin in its many forms that nails Jesus to the cross, but it is his mission to cleanse the place that

33

is reeking with sin and to make a place that is fragrant with sacrifice. The cross that is the outward sign of humanity at its worst he turns into the altar that is the outward sign of God at his best. There God the Son offers himself on our behalf to the Father who has sent him and, as he does so, releases into the human situation a totally new factor, the purifying power of his healing, renewing love and goodness which cleanses our humanity and indeed the whole created order and brings it back to God. As the ancient hymn puts it,

His the nails, the spear, the spitting, Reed and vinegar
  and gall,
From his patient body piercèd blood and water
  streaming fall:
Earth and sea and stars and mankind, by that stream
  are cleansèd all.

('Sing my tongue, how glorious battle glorious victory becomes' by Venantius Clementianus Fortunatus, from *Revised Church Hymnary*)

When the martyrs in Revelation are said to have washed their robes and made them white in the blood of the Lamb, the meaning is that they have joined themselves so closely to Christ that his life poured out on Calvary has covered their sin with his goodness, their unholiness with his holiness. So, at the Holy Communion we are bid to drink of the new covenant in his blood which is shed for many for the taking away of sin. We come stained, but he offers to us what he has first offered to the Father on Calvary, his own life that opens our lives up to God again and lets his renewing grace flow into us once more.

For as we look through the window of sacrifice, what we see is not just a long-ago Christ on a cross but a living

Christ whose sacrifice on the cross is still being offered to God on our behalf and has still power to do what it has always done; it still covers our sin with his goodness, our unholiness with his holiness. The letter to the Hebrews emphasises both that the sacrifice of the cross has been made 'once and for all' and never needs to be repeated, but also that the high priest who made that sacrifice is our contemporary who knows our situation, who is able to reach our sins with his cleansing, not by offering another sacrifice, but by ceaselessly offering to the Father what he did decisively and for ever on the cross. 'Because Jesus lives for ever, he has a permanent priesthood. Therefore he is able to save completely those who come to God through him, because he always lives to intercede for them' (7:24–5).

That verse suggests the biblical answer to the question that many people ask, 'How can the death of Jesus two thousand years ago make any difference to me today?' Since the one who died then is alive now, since the power to cleanse sin and cover our badness with his goodness remains his for ever, his sacrifice is as effective in our day for our sins as it was on the day when it was first offered. 'He is able to save completely those who come to God through him.'

One of the ways in which he comes to us is, as we have said, at the sacrament of Holy Communion where we are receiving afresh what he did for us on the cross. The emphasis is on the word 'receiving'. We are not just remembering his sacrifice in the sense of casting our minds back to a highly significant event in ancient history the way we might remember, say, the death of Socrates. The Holy Communion is not a sad memorial service for a long dead Jesus, although some of our traditions have threatened to make it so. For he is not dead – 'The Lord is here; his Spirit is with us.' At his table he offers us the bread and the wine through which he gives us his body and his blood, himself and his life once sacrificed on Calvary but now available to us to wash away our sins and fill us with the very same life and love that he poured out on Calvary long ago.

If we ask the New Testament what Christ is doing now one of its answers, given in the Hebrews verse that we have just quoted, is that he is interceding for us. Paul says the same thing in Romans 8:34. That is another way of saying that he is offering his once-made sacrifice to God on our behalf, not to persuade God to love us, for he has loved us from all eternity, but to provide the means by which God's love can reach us. Intercession is not about coaxing God to do things he is unwilling to do, it is about offering ourselves as the channels through which his love can be released to others.

God is self-giving love. From all eternity he lives in that love, the Father gives himself to the Son and the Son to the Father in the power of the Spirit. By that love we were made and by that love we are redeemed. God sends his Son into the midst of the mess of our world so that by his self-giving love that comes to its climax in the sacrifice of the cross, he may reach us and cleanse us with his forgiving grace and transforming Spirit.

God's love works where one person gives himself on behalf of another. That is what Jesus is doing on Calvary and that is what we are doing when we are caught up into his ministry of intercession and identify ourselves with some needy person or situation by offering our time, concern, faith and hope on their behalf so that through that intercession God's love may be able to do for that person and situation what by ourselves we cannot do.

The Scottish theologian, John McLeod Campbell, saw what Jesus was doing on Calvary as enacted intercession and lived out prayer. He gave himself to us utterly and completely by plunging into the depths of the mire of desolation and suffering that sin creates, and by offering himself on its behalf, opening it up to the cleansing that only God's love could give it. Into that offering we enter when we intercede 'through Jesus Christ our Lord', joining our feeble self-giving to his perfect self-giving to his Father for us all.

When we speak of sacrifice and intercession, we remind ourselves that this window on the cross is a church window, in other words, it sees what Jesus is doing as an act of worship, because at its heart worship is sacrifice; it is offering ourselves to God in union with Jesus. If the one sacrifice of Jesus has been effective in us, if our life has been joined to his and his life has entered ours, then we shall begin to follow him and to do what he is doing. We cannot and need not join him in offering the one sacrifice for sin, because he has offered that once for all on the cross, but, with him and in him, we can offer ourselves in worship to praise the name of the Father, to receive with obedient attentiveness the word of the Father, and to offer ourselves for others in interceding prayer to the Father.

Only the one sacrifice of Jesus can cleanse us from sin and we are day by day to continue to receive that cleansing. But, in and through the Christ who has so wonderfully offered himself for that cleansing, we are able to sacrifice ourselves in worship and daily obedience, to join him in offering ourselves in praiseful thanksgiving, in increasing commitment, in costly self-giving, so that his work may be done and the love by which he did all this may be made known and become mighty in the world for which he died.

Therefore, I urge you, in view of God's mercy to offer your bodies as living sacrifices, holy and pleasing to

God – this is your spiritual act of worship. Do not conform any longer to the pattern of this world, but be transformed by the renewing of your mind. Then you will be able to test and approve what God's will is – his good, pleasing and perfect will. (Romans 12:1–3)

POINTS TO PONDER

- In the light of the death of Jesus, think about the statement. 'Death is either the point of our final despairing or of our ultimate trusting.'

- How would you answer the question, 'How can the death of Jesus two thousand years ago make any difference to me today?'

- If intercession 'is not about coaxing God to do things he is unwilling to do but about offering ourselves as channels through which his love is released to others', what does this say to us about our own practice of intercessory prayer?

4

Justice

The fourth act of Shakespeare's *Merchant of Venice* can be read as a Christian drama of salvation. The story is well known; Antonio, the rich merchant, has pledged his money and, in default of that, his life to pay the debt of his friend Bassanio to Shylock the Jew, and the clever young lawyer Balthasar (Portia) has been hired to defend his life when he is unable to meet his financial obligations and Shylock is demanding his pound of flesh. Here indeed is a man who in love has pledged himself to lay down not just his money but his life for his friend.

Portia begins with her famous appeal to Shylock to show mercy, which in my day at school, we all learnt by heart, 'The quality of mercy is not strained' – an appeal which everyone in court that day is disposed to grant except Shylock to whom it is addressed. He, in spite of all pleas, insists, 'I will have my bond' and the judge has reluctantly to agree that it would be subversive of all good social order if mercy were allowed to bypass justice, if bonds and covenants freely entered into were allowed to be set aside because the consequences to one of the parties turned out to be dire.

The rest of the drama works out how mercy can prevail and justice still be done and it is that issue in the very different context of the cross of Jesus that we have to look at through this third of our windows on the cross. Through the first window we saw God's house and how at Calvary he brought his children into restored relationships with himself; through the second window we saw God's temple and the sacrifice that took away sins, but now we are in God's courthouse and are going to see how God's justice can be so administered that in his mercy sinners can be acquitted and made right with him.

The New Testament concern for the relationship between the cross of Jesus and the justice of God is particularly prominent in the teaching of St Paul, as for example in Romans 3:25–6 where he starts with the sacrifice in the temple and ends up with the verdict in the law court, 'God presented him [Jesus] as a sacrifice of atonement ... to demonstrate his justice at the present time, so as to be just and the one who justifies those who have faith in Jesus.' In what happens on the cross of Jesus God both demonstrates his justice and pronounces a positive verdict of 'not guilty' on those who have faith in Jesus. This and its meaning for us is what in this chapter we are trying to understand.

Instinctively of course we all warm to the thought of God as the dispenser of mercy and would prefer to think as little as possible about God as the dispenser of justice. That is because for most of us law courts are frightening places and even more because we know pretty well that if the strict standards of justice are applied to us as we are in ourselves, there is no possibility of a favourable verdict. We know very well that in God's court we are not the judges who decide or the lawyers who present the opposing arguments but the accused at the bar.

For that very reason, however, we shall be all the more interested in the proceedings in this court when we are promised that the verdict is the totally unexpected one of acquittal rather than the deserved one of condemnation and we shall be asking what God has done to make that possible and what we need to do to make it work for us.

40

In any case, in spite of our reluctance, it is important for us personally and for the whole of humanity, not just that mercy should be shown but that justice should be done. On the personal level, if I am simply forgiven a debt by someone to whom I owe money, I shall be left feeling, no doubt, grateful at the generosity shown me, but also uncomfortable and embarrassed at the memory of my failure; if however the amount I owed is paid on my behalf, then I shall be able to lift up my head and look the world in the eye again, because strict justice has been done and a wrong has not just been discounted but actually put to rights on my behalf. Precisely that is what God has done in Christ – not just forgiven or overlooked the wrong in his mercy, but taken decisive action to put it right again.

Also it is important to the whole of humanity that God should not be only the dispenser of mercy but the upholder of justice. One of the characteristics of the Christianity of the second half of the twentieth century is that it has rediscovered the passion for social justice that gripped prophets like Amos and Isaiah so strongly. We have become increasingly aware of the oppression and exploitation of the weak by the strong, of the poor by the rich, of the nations of the south by the nations of the north and have rediscovered the God who has a bias towards the poor and who will, in his dealings with nations and societies, turn against the tyrants and the oppressors and work to set all the captives free.

We have rejoiced in recent years to see that happen in eastern Europe and South Africa and have rejoiced with the militant maiden who sings in her Magnificat of the God who 'has brought down rulers from their thrones but has lifted up the humble. He has filled the hungry with good things but has sent the rich away empty' (Luke 1:52–3) and have prayed that he should go on doing it in

41

situations at home and abroad where all sorts of injustices still prevail.

To pray such a prayer is to invoke the God of justice of whom Paul speaks in Romans and it makes no sense to recognise his justice and to seek for it to be exercised towards oppressors in the world but to refuse to recognise and seek it when it is exercised towards sinners on the cross. In both cases it is the same God and the same justice that we are dealing with and in both cases it is not in conflict or contradiction with God's mercy and loving concern for his people, but is in fact the means by which he asserts and defends that mercy on behalf of all who are in need of it and against all who oppose it or stand in its way.

We sometimes think of God as if different parts of his nature were in conflict with each other, so that sometimes he is forgiving and sometimes he is implacable, sometimes he is the merciful Father who loves his people and sometimes he is the stern Judge assessing people in terms of abstract moral principles and a complicated set of rules about what is right and what is wrong.

To think like that is not to be in tune with the thinking of the Scriptures. It is not that sometimes God is just and sometimes he is merciful, as though he were like the man with the umbrella and woman with the parasol in the weather house, so that when justice is being displayed mercy is hidden and when mercy is being displayed justice is hidden. The God who speaks in the Scriptures is *both* just *and* merciful in everything that he does; the two are entirely consistent because the God who exercises both of them is entirely consistent with himself and faithful to himself and his purposes in all his works and ways.

That comes out clearly in the way the Old Testament prophets, and in particular Isaiah, speak of God's justice. He speaks for example of Jerusalem as the place 'once

full of fair judgement, where saving justice used to dwell'
(1:21). When he is looking forward to God's people
returning from exile he says to the anxious, 'Be strong,
fear not, your God is coming with judgement, coming
with judgement to save you' (35:4), and in the second
part of the book God identifies himself to the prophet,
'There is no God apart from me, a righteous God and
a Saviour' (45:21) where the meaning clearly is not 'a
righteous God and *in spite of that* a Saviour', but rather
'a righteous God and *therefore* a Saviour'.

Verses like that could be multiplied from the Psalms
and other Old Testament writings. We should not forget
either that in the Old Testament we have a book of Judges
which tells the story not of legal officials holding courts
and imposing sentences but of men and women God
raised up precisely to save and deliver his people from
the oppressing Philistines. All this serves to make the
point that in God righteousness and salvation, justice and
mercy, are not in conflict but are complementary descrip-
tions of how consistently and faithfully he pursues his
single purpose for his people and his world. In the God
who revealed himself in word to the prophets and even
more in the person and passion of Jesus Christ, mercy
is at the heart of justice, and his justice is his faithful
commitment to mercy.

God as Judge is not concerned with the upholding of
abstract ethical principles or the imposition of complicated rules of conduct, he is concerned with doing right
by his people, upholding his covenant with them so that
conditions are created in which they can fulfil his purposes
to rejoice in and serve him as their God and to reflect his
self-giving love in all their dealings with one another.

It is easy to see the Old Testament law as a series
of disconnected and largely outmoded regulations and
demands that God is making and the Ten Commandments

at the heart of the law as merely negative and forbidding. In the best insights of Judaism that Jesus shared, the law is seen not as an imposition but as a gift, the Maker's instructions about how to make our life in his world all that it was meant to be. The Ten Commandments are the fence round that good life warning us that if we stray beyond the boundaries into worship of idols, into lying, stealing, adultery and the rest we shall fall out with God and with one another and do harm to ourselves beyond our own repairing.

The positive heart of the law and of the love towards which it points and urges us is the two great commandments to love God and neighbour of which all the others are but specific applications and expressions. The justice of God consists in the maintenance of his commandments and the assertion and defence of his love. Since that is so, it is with confidence and joyful anticipation and not only with fear and trembling that we can proclaim, 'We believe that he shall come to be our Judge' – and put all things to rights in the judgements of his saving love.

But of course every positive implies a negative, and so here also; the more clearly we see that God in his justice is totally committed to the saving purposes of his love, the more clearly we shall also see that he is totally committed to the refusal and rejection of the situations and people who oppose and obstruct these purposes. When we were looking through the reconciliation window we saw that the negative side of God's love was his wrath and, now that we are looking through the justice window, we see the same thing in a different light, that the negative side of his judgement is his condemnation. If he is seriously set on the assertion and defence of his love, he will be just as seriously set on the rejection of everything and everybody that resists that love. To imagine that in our kind of world you can have the justice without the condemnation, the Yes of love without the No of rejection, is to collapse into an unthinking sentimentality that is at the end of the day not serious enough about anything to accept its consequences and see it through.

It is however basic to the New Testament gospel that God *is* serious about both his love and the justice that asserts and defends it, so that those who have failed to respond to that love and have embarked on ways of life that end up in the crucifixion of that love on a cross, when it becomes incarnate in Jesus, have to see themselves as standing under that condemnation. For Paul it is a condemnation that is pronounced on every one of us because in a thousand different ways 'all have sinned and fall short of the glory of God' (Romans 3:23).

In the same letter he describes in a succinct phrase the way in which that condemnation actually works itself out in practice, 'the wages of sin is death' (6:23). When human nature becomes self-centred rather than God-centred, when we set ourselves up as manufacturers of our own lifestyles and begin to ignore the Maker's instructions, there is in personal and social life conducted in that way an inbuilt destructiveness that sets people into life-eroding and ultimately fatal conflicts with one another, with their environment and internally with themselves. A godless society soon shows itself to be a society where divisions and wars abound, where the greed of the strong deals death to the natural environment and famine to the weak, and where all sorts of illnesses flourish from what is often a spiritual root in lives that are torn in pieces by stress, guilt and resentments of all kinds.

All these are what Paul calls the 'wages', the inbuilt consequences, of human sinning. The judgements of God do not mainly consist of his directing at us supernatural thunderbolts from heaven. To condemn sin he only needs to stand back and let us have our own way, because if we are left to ourselves, we shall destroy ourselves without his having to do anything about it at all. The judgement of God consists in letting sinful human nature have its own way and devise its own destruction. In the first chapter of Romans where Paul is speaking of how the wrath of God works out in human affairs he says no less than three times that 'God handed them over ... [to] the sinful desires of their hearts' (v. 24), to 'shameful lusts' (v. 26) and to 'a depraved mind' (v. 28), and if we have any insight into what is going on in our own society we shall see that these destructive forces that we go on letting loose are increasing their hold upon us day by day. The Christian values on which our society was built cannot resist them, once we have cut off these values from the source of their life by weakening or even severing our relationship with God. 'The wages of sin is death' is written not just on the boards that the religious fanatics carry on their backs in the high streets, but all over the contemporary world of which we are part.

But, thanks be to God, 'the wages of sin is death' is only half a verse and God's condemnation of sinners by handing them over to the consequences of their sinning can never be the last word. The verse continues and so does the gospel, 'but the gift of God is eternal life in Christ Jesus our Lord', where undeserved gift is in the sharpest contrast to earned wages and where freely given life is the undoing of the richly deserved death. The final goal of God's justice can never be condemnation; it is at its very heart saving justice, it is the means, as we have seen, by which he asserts his mercy on behalf of those who are in most need of it. Those who are in most need of it are certainly those who have rejected that mercy, crucified that love and involved themselves in the process of progressive disintegration that we have just been describing. It is for them, to deliver them from that death that is the wages of their sin, that God so loves the world that he gives his only Son that whoever believes in him should not perish but have eternal life (John 3:16).

But, if God's just love is to save without compromising its own integrity by indulging sinners in their sin in the process, what must be done, and what therefore was Jesus doing that put things right the day he died on Calvary? As Paul puts it how can God 'demonstrate his justice ... so as to be just and to justify those who have faith in Jesus' (Romans 3:26)?

Christian theologians have been pondering that question for two thousand years and have come up with a variety of answers, some of which we are looking at in other chapters and some of which we should consider here. Some have seen what Jesus did on the cross as offering God *compensation* for human sin, a kind of balancing of the books in which the suffering of Jesus to the death somehow pays for our sinning and his goodness makes up for our badness so that at the end of the day the accounts are squared and the debt is repaid. Such ideas lurk behind the verse of the familiar hymn, 'There is a green hill far away', 'There was no other good enough to pay the price of sin; He could only unlock the gate of heaven, and let us in.'

Such a view leaves us asking what kind of God it is who seeks that kind of compensation, who gives judgement in his court and decides how much he needs to be paid for the insult, injury and frustration he has suffered at our hands, who is working with some sort of moral calculus that can evaluate how much goodness it takes to cancel out how much badness. To introduce the notion of compensation in this connection inevitably brings artificiality and unreality into the discussion, and seems hard to square with the nature and character of the God that the gospel of Christ reveals to us.

An alternative explanation is to look at the cross not in the context of the civil courts and their concern with fixing compensation, but of the criminal courts with their concern for the just punishment of those who are found guilty before them. So it has often been taught that Jesus was punished for our sins instead of us and, because the punishment purges the convict of his crime, the justice of God has been satisfied and the case against us is closed. As another well-known hymn 'Man of sorrows' puts it,

> Bearing shame and scoffing rude,
> In my place condemned he stood,
> Sealed my pardon with his Blood,
> Hallelujah! what a Saviour!

We can all join in with the concluding Hallelujah, but nevertheless recognise the problems of thinking about what was achieved by Jesus on the cross in this way. Can we really think of God the Father imposing punishment on Jesus his well-beloved Son in whom he is always pleased? What kind of justice is it that lets anyone but the guilty criminal be punished for what he has done?

Convincing answers to these questions have been difficult to come by, although those who have looked at the cross in this way have tried hard to find them. Perhaps however we do not need to worry too much, since the idea of vicarious punishment, as is being increasingly recognised, is not prominent in the way the New Testament writers approach the cross.

What comes over from them is that what God wants to do is not so much to punish sin and the sinful human nature that goes on sinning, as to remove and eliminate them from the scene, so that they no longer frustrate his purposes, spoil his world and put his people into wrong relationships with himself and one another. He wants not so much to punish sin, but rather to nullify it and to rescue his people from it. His justice means that he cannot tolerate or compromise with wrong things and wrong people but his justice is above all a saving justice in which he administers his love and his mercy, and it seeks to rescue people from the wrong things around them and in them.

Paul puts what Jesus was doing on the cross into a single sentence in Romans 6:10, 'The death he died, he died to sin once for all; but the life he lives, he lives to God.' God in his saving justice seeks not compensation or retribution for sin, but the breaking of the grip and power of our destructive sinfulness. To do that Jesus, on whom sin has no grip or hold, because, unlike us, he has not sinned, comes to be the friend of sinners. He is that, not in any sentimental or superficial way, but by entering further and further into the destructiveness that sin causes, the physical pain, the treachery, the power-seeking, the cowardice, violence and cruelty that press sore upon him on Calvary and, worst of all, the alienation from God that makes him cry, 'My God, my God, why have you forsaken me?'

But God is just; because Jesus was right and did right in the eyes of his Father, there flows out from him the healing creativity that has healed the sick in Galilee, and that now is released on the cross. Just as sin has inevitably negative results in the destructiveness that leads to death, so goodness has positive results and releases the kind of creativity that brings new life even in the midst of death. The man who does right on the cross, who in the darkness of evil fulfils the law by loving the Lord his God with all his heart and mind and soul and strength and his neighbour, including his enemy, as himself, is the man from whose side, according to John 19:34, there flows blood and water: the blood of his costly obedience that rescues us from sin and recreates our relationship with God, and the water that in John's Gospel always stands for the new life that the Holy Spirit brings. The man who does right where everyone else is doing wrong, is able, in the justice of God, to rescue us from all that is wrong and to give us a new beginning by breaking our relationship to sin and bringing us into a new relationship with himself. God is just because he at last finds in Jesus a new humanity from which sin is eliminated and, in giving us Jesus, he gives us a new life that has died to the sinful past, that is right with God and that will do right by God in our dealings with one another. As Paul puts it, 'count yourselves dead to sin but alive to God in Jesus Christ' (Romans 6:11). In Jesus, and in those who receive Jesus, God's saving justice begins to have its way in his world.

When the great contemporary theologian, Karl Barth, was writing about the resurrection of Jesus he entitled the chapter, 'The Verdict of the Father'. In the law courts of Caiaphas and Pilate Jesus was unjustly condemned to die, but in his Father's supreme court to which in his dying breath he appealed, the verdict of the lower courts was quashed and replaced with the judgement of the Father, 'He shall live'. As Peter says to the Jews in Acts 2:23, 'You, with the help of wicked men, put him to death by nailing him to the cross. *But God* raised him from the dead'. In the reversed judgement of that 'But God' is all our hope, for that judgement applies not only to him, but to those who put their trust in him and on that saving justice, in life and in death, we all rely.

POINTS TO PONDER

- 'It is important to the whole of humanity that God should be not only the dispenser of mercy but the upholder of justice.' Do you agree?

50

- In the light of the cross how do you understand the statement, 'He shall come again to be our Judge'?

- What do you think Paul means by 'Count yourselves dead to sin but alive to God in Jesus Christ'? (Romans 6:11)

5

Freedom

Not long ago I heard a talk by an American theologian in which she was discussing what language it was appropriate for people at the end of the twentieth century to use when they were addressing God in prayer and worship. Being of a strongly feminist persuasion she explained to us that she herself had not used the word 'Lord' for many years because, in her ears at least, it savoured too much of male power and patriarchal domination.

Such remarks have become quite commonplace in recent years, but what caught my attention was the almost throw-away aside that immediately followed. 'Of course', she said, 'we have to be careful with our black sisters because in their tradition they still seem to like to talk about and sing to "the Lord." ' That set me thinking and asking why that should be so, and the answer I reached was that for them the dominant oppressor was the earthly slave-owning 'Massa', but the one to whom they looked for their liberation was the heavenly Lord. It was the Lord who told Moses to go down into Egypt's land with the message to oppressing Pharaoh, 'Let my people go'. They sang of that in the hope and expectation that he would do it again for them.

For the Afro-American slaves the Lord was not the oppressor but the liberator from oppression and I could not help feeling that her black sisters were far nearer the biblical understanding of God's Lordship than the sophisticated feminist who rejected the whole idea out of hand, without looking at the context in which it was originally set.

The divine name Yahweh which the English versions have nearly always translated as 'Lord' is, according to Exodus 3, revealed to Moses at the very moment when he is being sent into Egypt to get his people out of the slavery that they have endured so long. He is to give this name to the people, not as the name of yet another oppressor, all the more to be dreaded because he is divine, but as the name of the God who is about to take decisive action for their liberation, so that in his protection and care they can be led to a land of their own where they can be free.

Indeed in the verse that precedes the Ten Commandments God introduces himself as the giver of freedom, 'I am Yahweh your God who brought you out of Egypt, out of the land of slavery' (Exodus 20:1). He can claim their worship and obedience, not because he is stronger or even holier than they are, but because in their dire need, when they could not help themselves, he has proved his great love for them, by his great liberation of them. In the Passover meal the people remember with gratitude what he did for them long ago and look with hope and expectation for the same Lord to do the same thing against the tyrants, persecutors and oppressors of today.

The exodus from Egypt occupies in the Old Testament the central place that the death and resurrection of Jesus occupies in the New. By what he did in Egypt, by what he did on Calvary God shows his people who he is and what he is ready to do for them, and that action is always for their liberation. That note is struck right at the beginning of Luke's Gospel when Zechariah, the father of the newly-born John the Baptist, looks forward at what God is starting to do and sings, 'Praise be to the Lord, the God of Israel, because he has come to his people and set them free' (Luke 1:68). Notice again the conjunction 'Yahweh, the Lord . . . sets free'.

The same concern is expressed by Jesus himself in his sermon at Nazareth where he sets out, as it were, his prospectus for his ministry by making his own the words of Isaiah, 'He [the Lord!] has sent me to proclaim freedom for the prisoners' (Luke 4:18), and at the end of his ministry in the context of the Passover, with all its echoes of the exodus from Egypt, in his words over the chalice he says, 'This is my blood of the new covenant which is poured out for many for the forgiveness of sins' (Matthew 26:28). This is a crucial verse for what we can see of the cross through this window and it is worth looking more closely at it.

First we should note that here we are as close as we can be to the mind of Jesus on the eve of his crucifixion. If we cannot rely on Paul in 1 Corinthians and the first three Gospel writers when they report that Jesus said these words or something very like them on that last night with his disciples, then we should have to reach the conclusion that we know very little about him at all. These words have the highest claim to genuineness and we need to read them with the greatest respect and care.

Secondly we should note that the word *aphesis* which most of the English versions translate here as 'forgiveness' is in fact an important part of the vocabulary of liberation and the first preferred rendering of my New Testament Greek dictionary is 'release': 'My blood of the new covenant poured out for many *to release them from their sins.*' It is not just a matter of remitting the guilt of the past, but setting people free from their sins in the same complete way that God set his people free from Egypt long ago. This is what Jesus said he was doing when he died, a new exodus not from a land dominated by a tyrannical king, but from a life dominated by oppressing sin.

Thirdly we should note the reference to the shedding of blood in this verse. In the first exodus from Egypt the blood shed was that of the lamb that marked the doors of the Israelite houses and kept the angel of death at bay. As far as God is concerned Israel is set free by an exercise of sovereign power without any suggestion of cost or sacrifice to the one who exercises that power. But the exodus that inaugurates the new covenant is costly for the liberator. The blood that is shed now is the blood of Jesus, he has become the Lamb of God who takes away the sin of the world, our release from our sins is accomplished not by the easy action of an omnipotent divine hand but by the costly passion of the man who goes to the cross.

This brings us right into the heart of what the New Testament means by the word redemption. The English word comes from a Latin root that means 'buying back' and it translates two Greek verbs, *luein* and *sozein*, that mean to loose and to rescue. In the New Testament they always refer to a costly rescue, so costly that it takes nothing less than the blood of Jesus, which means his surrendered life, to accomplish it. As Peter puts it in his first letter, 'For you know that it was not with perishable things such as silver and gold that you were redeemed from the empty way of life handed down to you from your forefathers, but with the precious blood of Christ, a lamb without blemish or defect' (1 Peter 1:18–19).

According to Mark, Jesus himself saw his approaching death in the same terms when he said, 'The Son of man did not come to be served, but to serve, and to give his life as a ransom [*lutron*] for many' (Mark 10:45). The basic idea keeps recurring – freedom at great cost and we must explore it further now.

As Colin Brown puts it, 'Whenever men by their own fault or by some superior power have come under the control of someone else, and have lost their freedom to implement their will and decisions, and when their own resources are inadequate to deal with that other power, they can regain their freedom only by the intervention of a third party.'* In the ancient world there was a large group of people who were indeed under the complete control of someone else and had lost their freedom to implement their will and decisions – namely slaves. They could be freed only when the right price had been paid to their masters, and it was that transaction that the New Testament writers had at the back of their minds when they spoke of the ransom price that Christ has paid on the cross for our liberation.

Their common starting-point is that without Christ we are all slaves. We were made for freedom but we have lost that freedom and only through Christ can we get it back again. If we ask what it is that enslaves us the New Testament writers have a whole series of answers to offer. Paul tells us that, before we came to Christ, we were 'slaves to sin' (Romans 6:17–18), 'to the elemental spirits' (Galatians 4:3), 'to various passions and pleasures' (Titus 3:3). The writer to the Hebrews further extends the list by saying that Christ came to 'free those who all their lives were held in slavery by their fear of death' (Hebrews 2:15).

It is a very unflattering list and a diagnosis of the human situation that most of us are quite unwilling to accept. In the western world we like to think of ourselves as liber-

* 'Redemption' in *Dictionary of New Testament Theology*, vol. 3, p. 177.

ated people who are our own masters and who live in a democratic society where, within the limits of the law, we are free to do as we like and where the will of the majority of ordinary people is bound to prevail. Instead of confessing with Paul that we are the slaves of sin, we want to sing with the Victorian poet, 'I am the master of my fate, I am the captain of my soul.'

Before however we write Paul off we need to ask what he meant and whether what he says about us might not be disconcertingly more realistic and true to experience than some of the grand claims to freedom with which we seek to reassure ourselves.

Paul is not for a moment denying that every hour of every day we are making voluntary choices, after thought and consideration deciding to do one thing and not to do another, that these are our own decisions, not forced upon us by anybody and that we bear responsibility for them. To deny that would be to deny our humanity as people made in the image of God.

Nevertheless – and this is what Paul and the others mean by their talk of slavery – although that process of rational decision and responsible choice continues, it is affected through and through by the flawed people we have become and the flawed society to which we belong. We were created to love God first, our neighbour next and ourselves last – and this, as Jesus' two great commandments prove, is God's appointed order of priorities for his human creation. Our natural bent, however, leads us not to decide to observe that order but rather to reverse it by putting ourselves and our interests first, our neighbour a poor second and God a last resort. That reversal of priorities is a pretty good definition of sin. It is these reversed priorities that again and again knock our thinking askew, pull down our standards of right and wrong, incline us to act for our own interests even in defiance of the standards we recognise, and expose us to desires, greeds and habits that we may deplore and even detest but that we cannot control, with the result that again and again they have their way with us.

Paul means something like that when he says that we are slaves to sin. We are free to make our own decisions, but in making them we again and again show that we are under the mastery, not of God and his love and justice, but of our own interests and of a society that gives its allegiance to false gods and is in the process of bidding farewell to the God and Father of our Lord Jesus Christ and the values and priorities that spring from his gospel. We can decide in what ways we shall sin and, thank God, not everybody commits every sin, but the one thing that we cannot decide is not to be sinners.

Protestant theologians used to argue about whether we are sinners because we sin or whether we sin because we are sinners. At first sight it looks like a clever playing about with words to which such people are prone, but in fact it raises an important question. To say that we are sinners because we sin suggests that what is wrong with us is simply the wrong things that we do, but underneath the bad deeds there beats still a heart of gold that has it in its power to change its ways, to stop doing things that displease God and to start doing things that please him. That is a very optimistic picture that implies that our plight is not so serious after all. All we need to do is repent and reform and we might, on this showing, even be capable of saving ourselves without any need for what Jesus did for us on the cross.

On the other hand, to say that we sin because we are sinners paints a very much less rosy picture of human nature. On this view the trouble is not just in the things that we do but in the people that we are. Like Adam and Eve in the Genesis story, we, in solidarity with the whole human race, have broken with the God who made us and have chosen to be our own gods. We have constituted ourselves as the sole judges of good and evil and that has fundamentally altered our nature for the worse and constantly vitiates our thinking, our willing, our imaginations and our emotions. The basic sin in which we choose to obey ourselves rather than God has such a grip on us and has become such a part of us that we have become its prisoner and do not know how to shake ourselves free of it, even when we want to. In his pre-Christian days Paul had been a moral man all his life whose chief priority was to keep the law of God in every part and yet, as he looks back on that part of his life, he has to say of it,

> I know that nothing good lives in me, that is, in my sinful nature. For I have the desire to do what is good, but I cannot carry it out. For what I do is not the good I want to do; no, the evil I do not want to do – this I keep on doing. Now, if I do what I do not want to do, it is no longer I who do it, but it is sin living in me that does it. (Romans 7:18–20)

In that last sentence Paul is not denying responsibility for his actions, but concluding from hard experience of the moral struggle that again and again he has discovered that his sins are not the result of his choices, but his will is the unwilling prisoner of a power that he here calls sin that he has let into his life and that he now cannot expel. He is under enemy occupation and he cries out in his distress, 'What a wretched man I am! Who will rescue me. . . ?' And then, remembering that he has been rescued from himself and the sin that is in control of him, he immediately goes on, 'Thanks be to God – through Jesus Christ our Lord!' (Romans 7:24–5).

Jesus himself says the same thing in rather different terms when he speaks of the tree and its fruit.

'No good tree bears bad fruit, nor does a bad tree bear good fruit. Each tree is recognised by its own fruit. People do not pick figs from thorn-bushes, or grapes from briers. The good man brings good things out of the good stored up in his heart, and the evil man brings evil things out of the evil stored up in his heart.' (Luke 6:43–5)

The deeds we do are the result and expression of what is stored up in our hearts. A person with evil stored in his heart, corrupting the good that God put there the way poison corrupts good wine, has the same sort of problem as a thorn-bush that wants to bear figs; its basic nature needs to be changed and that is a task far beyond its own accomplishing. As Jesus put it to the highly moral churchman Nicodemus, 'You must be born again' (John 3:7).

So, you and I need to decide which of these two estimates of the human situation we are going to accept. Notice that in what he says Paul was not passing judgements on others, but reflecting honestly on his own past experience. We must do the same. To say that we are slaves to sin, before it can be a general statement about everybody, must first be a personal confession about ourselves in an area where self-deception is easy and honesty comes hard. But, looking steadily at ourselves in the light that streams from the cross of Jesus, can we say that we are fundamentally good people who have a few occasional lapses but are in full control of ourselves and free to change our ways whenever we decide to do so?

Or could it be that we have to come clean with ourselves and with God and confess that there is something deeply wrong at the heart of us that affects the way we think, act and feel? In all that we do we are under the pressures of bad habits and evil desires inside and of social pressures outside that drive us further and further away from God and that we do not know how to break or control. In other words we are slaves to sin who cannot set ourselves free.

Pride and self-esteem try hard to find reasons to protest against such a humbling confession, but in my honest moments, even if with the greatest reluctance, I have to admit that Paul's diagnosis fits my record all too accurately. Jesus has got it right as far as I am concerned; the disease is not just in the fruit but in the whole tree. I can rightly be described as a slave to sin because I have lost the freedom to be and to do what in my best moments I want to be and do and I know from long experience that on my own I do not know how to get it back again.

To people like that Jesus from the cross offers his gift of freedom. The supreme paradox of Calvary is that of all the people involved, only the man hanging on the central cross is free. The Jewish priests are not free; they are there to worship God and keep his laws, but they are so caught up in their shabby intrigues and the defence of their own interests that they cannot do these things. Pilate is not free; he is there to maintain Roman justice but he is under such pressures that he cannot do it and ends up being an accomplice in what he knows to be an act of gross injustice. The crowds who bay for Barabbas to be released and Jesus to be crucified are not free but are being irrationally driven by a worked-up mob hysteria that is incapable of seeing what the real issues are. The robbers on either side of Jesus are not free; their crimes have at last caught up with them and are now about to destroy them.

But Jesus on the cross is a free man among these slaves to their different forms of human sin. Crucifixion was the punishment meted out to runaway slaves, but here hanging among the slaves is their great liberator. When the man on the other cross, very nearly mastered by approaching death, turns to him and says, 'Jesus, remember me, when you come into your kingdom,' he is given an immediate certificate of emancipation, 'Today you will be with me in paradise' (Luke 23:40–3).

Jesus on the cross is free and can set others free – but that remains a great paradox. He is obviously not free to do anything he likes; he remains totally unresponsive to the taunting demands of his enemies that he should come down from the cross. Nevertheless he is free; he is there not by external compulsion or tragic accident, but because this is where he wants and needs to be in order to fulfil the purpose for which he came. In John's Gospel he says, 'The reason my Father loves me is that I lay down my life – only to take it up again. *No-one takes it from me, but I lay it down of my own accord*' (John 10:17–18, italics mine). It is his free embracing of his death that gives it its infinite value and turns his imposed martyrdom into his voluntary sacrifice.

In dying as he dies Jesus is free to be who he came to be and to do what he came to do. Under the most intense pressures from all the enslaving evils that are our undoing, his inner agony and humiliation, all the destructive forces of hatred, sin and death that are having their way with him, he remains free to love the Lord his God with all his heart, soul, mind and strength and to give himself in love for his neighbour and his enemy. Precisely when he is nailed helpless on the cross he is supremely free to serve his God and his people.

As we see him there, we begin to see that his kind of freedom is the only kind worth having. Like Adam and Eve in the story we long to be free *from* God and become our own masters. Eventually like them we discover that we have become slaves to all sorts of destructive forces that possess us and tear us apart. The truth is that we are free to be ourselves and to fulfil the purpose of our lives only when, like Jesus, we are free *for* God. Richard of Chichester was on to the secret when he prayed, 'In your service is perfect freedom' as was Horatius Bonnar when he sang, 'Make me a captive, Lord, and then I shall be free.' Paul delighted in being a slave not of sin but of Christ, because he had discovered that being bound to Christ was to begin to share in what he called 'the glorious liberty of the children of God' that would bring back freedom to humanity and ultimately through them to the whole created order (Romans 8:20–2).

We look at Jesus on the cross, the victim of all the evil bondages that imprison and destroy people and that have made his enemies imprison and destroy him. But in the midst of the agony, love is free to be itself and to do its loosing and redeeming work. Love is free even when it is still bound by sin and death but on the third day love will break all these bonds and burst out into total freedom.

He is free and he promises freedom; he comes to us in all the prisons of wrong thinking, wrong attitude, wrong priorities, wrong actions, the chains with which, out of long habit, we have bound ourselves, and the chains that the fallen society that has shaped us has forged for us. His word is, 'If the Son sets you free, you will be free indeed' (John 8:36). 'When I come, my freedom comes with me; there is nothing you have done or been in the past from whose guilt and power I cannot release you; there is no habit, no fear whose hold over you I cannot break, no situation so frustrating and destroying that I cannot show you how to receive God's love and do him service in it. Amidst sin and suffering I was free and opened the door to freedom and I can do it again for you.'

From slavery to sin to freedom for God – that is the road along which the crucified Jesus offers to take us and promises to lead us. If we will admit our bondages in his presence and invite him into the places where we feel most imprisoned and helpless, we shall test his claims and begin to taste his freedom as many have before us. It was such liberation that Wesley celebrated in his song of freedom 'And can it be . . ?',

> Long my imprisoned spirit lay
> Fast bound in sin and nature's night;
> Thine eye diffused a quickening ray –
> I woke, the dungeon flamed with light;
> My chains fell off, my heart was free.
> I rose, went forth and followed Thee.

POINTS TO PONDER

- How does what Jesus has done on the cross and goes on giving to us in Holy Communion actually release us from our sins?

- Are we sinners because we sin or do we sin because we are sinners? What difference does it make?

- 'Jesus on the cross is free and can set others free.' What do you think this means for him and for us?

6

Suffering

To reach our next window we have to leave the ancient wings of the house that go back to New Testament times, and enter the modern wing to look through a couple of windows that have been renovated and enlarged in our own day. The view of the cross that we get through them is specially significant for contemporary people and the questions that they ask. Note well, we did not construct these windows; people have looked through them down the centuries, but we have renovated and enlarged them, because we live near them and look through them more than we look through some of the others, because they show us what we need and want to see.

That has both advantages and dangers. Anything that makes the message of the cross real and relevant in a world where it is often ignored or misunderstood is to be welcomed. Nevertheless when we start saying things about the meaning of the death of Jesus that the New Testament writers do not say so directly and clearly, we need to ask how what we are saying is compatible with what they are saying and how the two are related to each other. That applies especially to the first modern window that we are approaching now.

James Shillito, the poet of the battlefields of the First World War, puts into moving words what is to be seen here. His poem 'Jesus of the Scars' begins,

65

> If we have never sought, we seek thee now;
> Thine eyes burn through the dark, our only stars;
> We must have sight of thorn-marks on thy brow,
> We must have thee, O Jesus of the scars.

and ends,

> The other gods were strong; but thou wast weak;
> They rode, but thou didst stumble to a throne;
> But to our wounds only God's wounds can speak,
> And not a god has wounds, but thou alone.

You have only to read these words to realise what an immediate and powerful appeal they make to us, because we are men and women of the twentieth century which has been dominated by an awareness of and horror at all the different kinds of suffering that afflict humanity and that people inflict on one another. In the seventeenth century the great theological question that haunted people's minds at the time of the Reformation was 'How can sinful people be reconciled to a holy God?' and so they were vitally interested in the answers that were given to that question not only by popes and Reformers but even more by Paul and the other New Testament writers and that we have been summarising in our chapters on Reconciliation, Justice and Freedom.

In our days these often seem to be answers to questions that people are not asking because we are not nearly as aware of our sins as we are of our sufferings; we see ourselves not as the villains who perpetrate evil, but as the victims who have to endure it and the question we are asking is, 'How can we believe in a God of love or in any God at all in a world where people endure such massive and undeserved affliction, in war, in famine, in natural disaster, in human abuse, exploitation and sheer neglect?'

For an answer to that question Shillito in his poem turns to the cross and finds there what, he claims, cannot be found anywhere else in the whole diverse world of religion, a God who does not hold himself aloof from the suffering of his people, or offer them sympathy and compassion from the safe immunity of his heavenly glory, but who in his love plunges from his height to our depths and at a specific historical moment becomes for a crucified world the man on the other cross. The uniqueness of Jesus is not in the loftiness of his teaching, the immaculate holiness of his life, the supernatural power of his miracles, his ability to bring pardon and a new quality of life to those who believe in him, but rather in his scars, in his sharing in our sufferings.

In order to make his point that Jesus reveals to us a God who suffers with us, Shillito has to affirm the divinity of Jesus, his identity with God. If he is just another man whom human jealousy and injustice combine to destroy, then he is just another innocent victim among millions of others and he can offer us no more than an example of how to suffer without being bitter with those who cause your suffering. If however his wounds are God's wounds then, in a way that the poem does not specify, they 'speak' to us in our own woundedness, there is a promise of something good coming out of our sufferings if the power that bears ultimate responsibility for the whole created universe brings all his goodness and love into the midst of everything that hurts and destroys.

It is fascinating to see how what a poet grasped intuitively in response to the atrocities of the First World War a theologian thought through in response to the atrocities of the Second. In his significantly titled book *The Crucified God*, the German theologian Jürgen Moltmann says that his intention is to do theology after Auschwitz and to ask the question, 'What can we say in defence of a

God who made a world in which the gas chambers of Auschwitz can be erected and who does nothing to stop the slaughter?'

The question with which Moltmann comes to the cross of Jesus shows that there has been a great reversal of approach from the traditional concerns that we have been examining in previous chapters. They asked, 'How can the ways of sinful humanity be put right before a God of holy love?' whereas Moltmann is voicing the modern question, 'How can the ways of a God of holy love be justified before a suffering humanity?' In the one case Christ stands to plead our cause before the judgement seat of God, in the other he stands to plead God's cause before the judgement seat of an abused and tortured humanity. In one case we are the villains and in the other the victims.

Before we are finished we shall have to ask whether and how far this new approach is a legitimate variation on the central theme of the gospel, but in the meantime we can explore some of its implications and the until now hidden facets of Calvary that it exposes.

For firstly, this fresh approach says new and important things about God, not least that he is capable of being exposed to and bearing the kind of pain and suffering that are an inseparable part of the human lot. For Moltmann as for Shillito, it is the person of God the Son who hangs on the cross and experiences excruciating physical pain and the spiritual dereliction that makes him cry to his Father, 'My God, my God, why have you forsaken me?' It is God the Son who undergoes human death and enters the mystery of all that lies beyond it. All that is involved in being, as the title of his book designates Jesus, *The Crucified God*.

For many non-Christian religious traditions such a thought is at best foolishness and at worst blasphemy. For

Greek philosophers like Plato a God who was weak and vulnerable to attack by beings lesser than himself, who was subject to death and dissolution rather than remaining changeless in eternity, was a contradiction in terms and no God at all. For Muslims to suggest that Allah, who is in sovereign control of all that happens, could become the helpless victim of his creatures and so subject to pain and death was the ultimate blasphemy. It is no accident that according to the Koran, the Spirit of God flees from Jesus before he is crucified, because he is the Spirit of a God who cannot be touched by suffering or become prey to death.

Even for traditional Christian thinking the idea of a God who suffers has often been a hard thought to contemplate. At this point the Christian doctrine of God has often been heavily influenced by the ideas of the Greek philosophy in terms of which it was originally formulated and has taught that God was 'impassible' which means not only that he is by nature incapable of suffering, but that he cannot be acted upon or influenced by anything outside himself and remains untouched and unmoved in his divine invulnerability.

Such teaching has always been hard to square with the fundamental Christian affirmation of the divinity of Jesus, that it was in fact one who bore this impassible divine nature who lay helpless in Mary's arms in Bethlehem and suffered dreadfully and was put to death at the hands of his human creatures. Theologians down the centuries have tried to have it both ways by saying that Jesus shared both the divine nature that could not suffer and the human nature that could, so that on the cross he suffered as man but as God he remained free from suffering. This may be ingenious but it is quite unsatisfactory, because it seems to tear Jesus into two parts with opposite qualities, a humanity that suffered and a divinity that could not suffer. If it was one whole person who was crucified, then either he suffered what that involved in every part of him or he did not; we shall have to come down on one side or the other, it is imposisble to have it both ways.

Many theologians of our own day, of whom Moltmann is typical, have said that to know what God is like, we should not start from general statements about the divine nature being incapable of suffering, but rather find out what he is like from looking at Jesus and what he said and did because 'Anyone who has seen me has seen the Father' (John 14:9). If that is our starting-point we shall find ourselves saying, also with John, not that God is impassible but that God is love (1 John 4:8). To say that he is love is to say, not that he is impassible, but that he is passionate, not that he rules over us in aloofness but that he cares for us with a depth of emotion far beyond our imagining. Love, far from being detached from the one it loves, is totally involved, rejoicing when those it loves are well and do well, grieving and angry when they are harmed or harm themselves. Love is vulnerable to those it loves, it laughs with those who laugh, it weeps with those who weep, it hastens to those who are hurt and longs, like a mother with her child, to save them from that hurt by bearing it, if it can, in their stead.

Such is the God who reveals himself in the Christian Scriptures, the one who is in himself love, who has in the freedom of that love made a world and a humanity to receive and to return that love, who has entered into convenant love with Israel and involved himself passionately in all the history of his people. Now, seeing them and the world to which they belong plunged in the misery that results from their refusal to live in and by his love, in the passion of his love he gives his only Son to share that misery and to make a way out from it by himself becoming man and plunging to the depths of human misery on the cross.

The God of the Bible and supremely the God of the cross is not so shut up in his majesty and imprisoned by his divinity that he cannot enter into the life of his creatures and endure what needs to be endured on their behalf, so that his good purposes for them may be fulfilled. The bit of truth in the teaching about God's impassibility is that God, because he is God, cannot be *forced* or *compelled* to do anything by anything or anybody outside himself. There is nothing that we can do to make him love us, come to us, die for us. He loves us, because, being who he is, he has *chosen* to love us, *chosen* to care for us, *chosen* to come to us, *chosen* to share our suffering and be subject to our death. Because he is God, he is free, but, because he is the God and Father of Jesus, he is love, and in the freedom of that love he has chosen to make our suffering his own.

Moltmann goes further and interprets God's suffering in a trinitarian way by distinguishing between the suffering of the Father and the suffering of the Son. When human suffering and death are taken into the life of God, they affect the Father and the Son in two different ways; the Son has to bear the pain and die the death, but the Father has, while his Son is suffering and dying, to stand by helplessly and allow it all to happen. God knows not only what it is like to suffer, but also what it is like to watch the one you love best suffer and be unable to do anything about it; what it is like to mourn when his Son is separated from him by death. As Moltmann himself puts it, 'To understand what happened between Jesus and his God and Father on the cross, it is necessary to talk in trinitarian terms. The Son suffers dying, the Father suffers

71

the death of the Son. The grief of the Father here is just as important as the death of the Son.'*

It is not hard to see that such an approach has an immediate pastoral appeal, because it establishes a close connection between the life of God and those who suffer and die, as well as with those who have to watch over the suffering and mourn the death of those they love greatly. That is why this window on the cross attracts many who would not understand nearly so easily what was to be seen through some of the others.

Nevertheless we have to ask how this whole approach, however congenial we may find it, relates to the biblical case from which it starts and which it claims to be interpreting. The nearest that the New Testament comes to what Moltmann teaches about the grieving and mourning of the Father is in Romans 8:32 where Paul says that God 'did not spare his only Son but gave him up for us all', thus comparing God's sacrifice of Jesus with Abraham's sacrifice of Isaac on Mount Moriah, as recounted in Genesis 22, and at least hinting and implying that God's anguish in having to go through with his sacrifice was even greater than Abraham's who at the last minute had his son spared.

Whatever we may think of that, it is a pretty flimsy base on which to declare so confidently that the grieving of the Father is just as important as the dying of the Son. To be fair to Moltmann, he would not attempt to base his case on particular texts but claim rather that it was a fair deduction from what the Bible says about the passionate love of God. Such a God with such a love could not but grieve and mourn to behold his Son writhing in agony on the cross and bowing his head in death. Nevertheless Moltmann goes well beyond the New Testament in draw-

* *The Crucified God* (London, SCM, 1974), p. 243.

ing that implication and we need to ask ourselves how far we can join him in laying such emphasis on an aspect of the matter, however comforting, that the Bible does not explicitly mention at all.

Whatever we may think about that intriguing teaching of the suffering of the Father along with but distinct from the suffering of the Son, the main point stands – there is good New Testament ground for believing that on the cross God in Jesus is himself bearing human suffering, provided that we immediately add that he who shares our suffering also overcomes it. He comes to us in our suffering, not just to say, 'You are not alone, I am with you in all this', but also to say, 'My presence with you on the cross is my promise that, however meaningless all this may seem now, I will not help you to endure it, but will make it a way by which you can come to an unimaginable and unexpected renewal of life beyond it.'

To meet the penitent thief Jesus had to hang on the other cross beside him, but, when the man turned to him there, he did not say only, 'Today I am with you on Calvary' but also 'Today you will be with me in paradise.' The sight of Jesus with us in our pain is the promise of our healing; the sight of Jesus sharing our death is the promise of our life. The Jesus of the scars, whom Shillito rightly sees that we need, is the Jesus who three days later will show his disciples these scars as the trophies of his victory and the badges of his resurrection.

The gospel of the cross is not about the glorification of suffering, but about its transformation. The cross of Jesus is the vehicle that carried him to his resurrection. Therefore our hope, when we are suffering, is that he will take us on that journey with him. If he is to be of any help to us, we must know not only that he is in it with us but that he knows how to make what looks a one-way street to death a highway to new life.

To take a homely example: if you are about to go
into hospital for a dreaded operation for a serious and
dangerous complaint there are two kinds of friends who
will be of little use to you. The first is the hale and hearty
fellow who has never had a day's illness in his life. If he
slaps your back and says, 'I'm sure you will soon be fine,'
it does not mean a thing, because he does not know what
he is talking about. The second is the chronic invalid
who has the same illness and has been through the same
operation and is no better after it than before it. His
gloomy message can only be, 'It did not work for me and
I don't expect it will work for you either.'

There is however a third kind of friend who can help
and encourage greatly. He has been just as ill as you are
now, he has dreaded the operation and found it an ordeal,
but he has come through it and counted it all well worth
enduring because he has made a full recovery. That is the
friend whose company you will seek and on whose words
you will hang.

Jesus is that third friend. As the Scottish metrical version of Hebrews puts it,

> Though now ascended up on high,
> he bends on earth a brother's eye,
> partaker of the human name,
> he knows the frailty of our frame.
>
> Our fellow-sufferer yet retains
> a fellow-feeling of our pains;
> and still remembers in the skies
> his tears, his agonies and cries.
>
> In every pang that rends the heart
> the Man of Sorrows had a part,
> he sympathises with our grief
> and to the sufferer sends relief.

We need to know both these things about him, first, that he knows from the inside the full horror of human suffering in all its aspects and so is indeed our brother when we suffer; but also that he has made a way through suffering and death to life in all its fullness and is therefore in a position to say to us, 'In this world you will have trouble. But take heart! I have overcome the world' (John 16:33).

Christ has both hung on the crucifix that numbers him among the world's victims, but also sits on the throne where the scars are not left behind but rather transformed into 'rich wounds yet visible above in beauty glorified.' The pain becomes in him the raw material out of which the glory is fashioned and his promise is that it may be so for us also. A God who has the glory without the pain, and a God who is as overcome as we are by the pain are alike inadequate. It is the crucified Lord who reigns through, from, and as a result of his cross who can offer hope to all who suffer and in their suffering look to him. Out of what in itself is so senseless and meaningless Christ can fashion a glory that transforms and makes beautiful all the ugly and destroying things that have happened to us.

Those who long for and speak of miraculous healings and dramatic deliverances from evil, need to remember the logic of Calvary, the good news of the God who achieves his purposes with us, not only, or perhaps even mainly, when he takes us *out* of suffering but even more when he takes us the way Christ went *through* suffering and death to life and glory. The God and Father of our Lord Jesus Christ does not send or organise our sufferings, but the cross is his demonstration of how he can conquer it, not by abolishing it, but by using it to fulfil his purposes as he did on the cross for his Son – no immediate relief, but on the third day resurrection from the dead! If we ask God how he justifies himself in the face of the world's agony, he will point us to his Son in whom his own passionate love broke through into the heart of that agony, shared it with us and made it a way to his Father's life and glory. His love shines from his cross and he invites us to see and trust it there.

Through the other windows we saw Jesus as the Saviour of those who perpetrate evil: through this window we see him as the Saviour of those who are the innocent victims of evil. Peter in his letter speaks of Christ as himself the innocent victim who 'committed no sin and no deceit was found in his mouth' (1 Peter 2:22 quoting Isaiah 53:9), so that there is a good scriptural basis for believing that he has much to say and to give to all other innocent victims whose suffering is inflicted upon them undeserved.

That said, it is still important to recognise that the New Testament writers concentrate on what he did for the sinners rather than what he did for the sufferers, and to keep true to the biblical balance, we must be careful when we are looking through this window, not to forget what we have already seen through the others. We must not focus so exclusively on our need for help in our sufferings that we forget our even greater need for release from our sins, which are the cause of a great deal of the suffering to others and to ourselves.

At the end of the day the perpetrators of evil and their victims are not two separate groups with different people belonging exclusively to each. Those who do evil to others are often the victims of the evil that others have done to them; those who in one aspect of their lives are victims needing sympathy and justice are often in other parts of their lives sinners needing pardon and release. The contemporary debate about whether young criminals are villains responsible for their own actions or the product of broken homes, unemployment and an unjust and uncaring society cannot be won by either side. The truth is that they are both: the villains are the victims, and the victims have it in them to be the villains.

If that is so, we all stand in need of all that the crucified Christ has to offer, his scars offer solace and hope to all to whom life has been cruel and destructive, but also pardon and acceptance to all who have sinned against neighbour and against God. 'He was despised and rejected by men, a man of sorrows and familiar with suffering . . . Surely he took up our infirmities and carried our sorrows . . . But he was pierced for our transgressions, he was crushed for our iniquities; the punishment that brought us peace was upon him, *and by his wounds we are healed*' (Isaiah 53:3–5, italics mine).

POINTS TO PONDER

- How would you answer Moltmann's question, 'What can we say in defence of a God who made a world in which the gas chambers of Auschwitz can be erected and who does nothing to stop the slaughter?'

- Do you think Moltmann's teaching about a Son who shares our suffering and a Father who mourns over his Son's suffering and death is helpful to people who are themselves in the midst of suffering and mourning?

- 'The villains are the victims and the victims have it in them to be the villains.' Is this true?

Victory

Still in the modern wing of the house, we move to our next window and notice that it has two swords emblazoned on either side of it and over it a banner on which there is portrayed what can only be described as a fierce looking lamb! This is a military window through which we see the cross as the historic battlefield where good fights with evil, where Jesus the Lamb of God encounters the massed forces of his enemies and wins his decisive victory over them all.

The window is rightly placed in the modern wing of the house. It has been a highly favoured way of looking at Calvary ever since it came to new prominence in the book *Christus Victor* – Jesus the Conqueror – written by the Swedish theologian Gustav Aulén in 1930 and still with a good claim to be considered the most influential book about the cross to be produced in the twentieth century.

The reasons for its popularity are not too hard to understand. Most people today are not familiar with temple sacrifices, ancient slave markets or Jewish law courts, from all of which, as we have seen, the New Testament writers derived the words and ideas they used in speaking of the cross. But everybody in our century knows about war and in the generation in which *Christus Victor* was written, most people either had been caught up in one war or were afraid that they were about to be caught up in another. World wars in our century have been the events that have decided the destinies of nations, families and individuals, and if we see the cross of Jesus as having the same critical significance for people, for nations and for the future of the world, it is a very easy step to speak of it also in terms of warfare and battle, defeat and triumph.

It is therefore no accident that both our modern windows on the cross point to the two central experiences that war brings to people; on the one hand suffering and death, the subject of our last chapter, and on the other defeat and victory, the subject of this. With Shillito we want to know that Christ is with us when we are the casualties of the battle, but we also want to know that in Christ there is assurance of final victory over all our enemies.

The cross of Jesus, like war itself, has both a passive and an active side to it. It is both something that is done to him, of which he is the helpless victim, but – and this is what comes specially into focus through this new window – it is also decisive action, something that in his suffering and his death he achieves which has in it the power to change everything for everybody for ever; it is not just his passion, it is his victory.

That is the point that John is making, when, at the end of his story of the crucifixion in which he goes out of his way again and again to make it clear that Jesus is in control of everything that is happening, he records in John 19:30 his last word, as he bows his head and dies, the triumphant shout, *Tetelestai*, which means not so much, 'It is finished,' in the sense that 'The worst is over, it is all behind me now,' as 'It is accomplished, the battle has been fought to its desired conclusion; there is nothing left to do because the victory has been won.'

John strikes the same note as he introduces the crucifixion story with the words of Jesus in chapter 12 in which he first says that the final outcome of all that is about to happen is that the Father will be glorified (12:28), the evil forces that have dominated the life of the world defeated and the whole of humanity drawn to Jesus, ' "Now is the time for judgement on this world; now the prince of this world will be driven out. But I, when I am lifted up from the earth, will draw all men to myself." He said this to show the kind of death he was going to die' (12:31–3). A right famous victory indeed!

It is obviously of considerable symbolic significance to John that being crucified involved being 'lifted up from the earth'. It is a phrase that he uses several times in this connection; the suffering victim is at the same time the reigning king, the cross is the throne that raises him up to a level above all others. It is not going too far to say that in that phrase John is inviting us to look simultaneously at Jesus lifted up on the cross to die, lifted up from the dead to live and lifted up to the right hand of the Father to reign. It is not so much that the suffering comes first and then three days later the victory that gives the suffering its meaning. For John the suffering and the victory, the cross and the throne belong so closely together that you cannot have the one without the other. On the cross Jesus is already putting to rout all the forces of evil that have attacked him; and the resurrected Jesus still has wounds in his hand and his side. His suffering is not without the signs of glory dawning, his glory is not without the signs of suffering endured.

In almost exactly the same way the writer of the book of Revelation is shown in his vision 'a Lamb, looking as if it had been slain, standing in the centre of the throne' (5:6), who is introduced also as 'the Lion of the tribe of Judah, the root of David, [who] has triumphed' (5:5). In the strength of that victory he receives the praise of the whole creation, 'Worthy is the Lamb, who was slain, to receive power and wealth and wisdom and strength and honour and glory and praise' (5:12). The lion and the lamb have not only lain down together, as Isaiah prophesied, they have become one in Christ, who is both lion-like Lamb and lamb-like Lion, the fierce Lamb who is both the victim of and the victor over all his foes. The way in which all the New Testament writings ascribed to John emphasise Christ's work as victorious conflict with his enemies can be summed up in the words of 1 John 3:8, 'The reason the Son of God appeared was to destroy the devil's work.'

In the Pauline letters the note of victory after battle is sounded clearly in Colossians 2 where, after noting how Christ forgave us by nailing to his cross all the accusations that the law could muster against us, he goes on, 'And having disarmed the powers and authorities, he made a public spectacle of them, triumphing over them by the cross' (2:15). The reference is to a victorious Roman general leading his captives through the streets of his city for all the citizens to see as evidence of his complete victory over them. This, according to this passage, is what Christ has done to those Paul describes as 'powers and authorities', whose identity we must look at in a moment, and provides evidence in what results from the cross that he and not they have won the day.

We can also think of how Paul ends his great resurrection chapter in 1 Corinthians 15, where he is thinking of the foe that Christ has defeated as the death that is the consequence of sin and bursts into what might be called a song of taunting triumph, 'Death has been swallowed up in victory. Where, O death is your victory? Where, O death, is your sting? The sting of sin is death, and the power of sin is the law. But thanks be to God! He gives us the victory through our Lord Jesus Christ' (15:54–7). Here the defeated foes are not the mysterious principalities and powers of Colossians but the unholy triad of death, sin and law, and it is made clear that Christ's victory is one that we share – 'He gives *us* the victory'.

We have adduced enough New Testament evidence to show that the cross has been looked at from this point of view right from the start and, even if it is not a major theme like some we have already looked at, it has a much more secure grounding in the biblical texts than that of Christ's sharing of our suffering that we looked at in the last chapter. The moderns may have enlarged this window and, for the reasons we have already indicated, made much more of this theme than previous generations, but the window itself has always been in place and has often been looked through in the past.

In his book Aulén traces how this theme has been developed down the Christian centuries in the theology of the Church, but it has also kept appearing in its hymnody. In the sixth century Venantius Fortunatus celebrated the victory of Christ on the cross in words we still use,

> Sing, my tongue, the glorious battle,
> Sing the last, the dread affray;
> O'er the cross, the victor's trophy,
> Sound the high triumphal lay:
> How, the pains of death enduring,
> Earth's Redeemer won the day.

Nearly a thousand years later Martin Luther, who among the Reformers spoke most often of Christ's cross as his victory, reminds us that

> With force of arms we nothing can,
> Full soon were we down-ridden;
> But for us fights the proper man
> Whom God himself hath bidden.

In the nineteenth century Newman celebrates how

When all was sin and shame,
A second Adam to the fight,
And to the rescue came.

And expresses his wonder that in Christ the very

... flesh and blood,
Which did in Adam fail,
Should strive afresh against the foe,
Should strive and should prevail.

In our day we can think of some of the songs that have emerged from the Marches for Jesus in which Christians have sought to celebrate the triumph of Christ in the streets of our towns and cities, but from my own Scottish background I have cherished a less generally known hymn that exactly catches the same motif,

Our Lord Christ hath risen, the Tempter is foiled,
His legions are scattered, his strongholds are spoiled,
O sing Hallelujah, Be joyful and sing,
Our foes are all vanquished, Christ Jesus is king.

('Our second Christ hath risen' by William Plunket,
from *Revised Church Hymnary*.)

It is perhaps no accident that as we look through this window we should be quoting the songs of many Christian centuries, because what we see here is, of all the ways of approaching the cross, the one that most moves us to exuberant praise, and rightly so. But exuberant praise, far from being an alternative to careful thinking, should be an incentive to it and as we sing our hymns standing in front of this window, there are also three questions that we need to ask. Who are the enemies that Jesus took on and defeated at Calvary? What was it that won the victory there? What are the consequences of that victory for us today?

From our Scripture passages we have already had indications as to the identity of the enemies that Christ took on and vanquished on the cross. It can be said of his enemies what Paul said of ours, 'Our struggle is not against flesh and blood, but against the rulers, against the authorities, against the powers of this dark world and against the spiritual forces of evil in the heavenly realms' (Ephesians 6:12).

In all the New Testament writings there is an awareness that behind the human perpetrators of the crucifixion, Judas, the Jewish priests, the Roman governor and soldiers, there are lurking in the background shadowy spiritual forces who are using human agents to foil God's redemptive purposes. Paul refers to them again in 1 Corinthians, 'None of the rulers of this age understood it [God's secret wisdom], for if they had, they would not have crucified the Lord of glory' (2:8). They thought they were using human agents to frustrate God's purpose, but in fact they were themselves being used to fulfil it.

This awareness of the spiritual enemies with whom Jesus was locked in deadly conflict right through his ministry, is apparent not only in the particular accounts of how on specific occasions people were delivered from binding and destructive spiritual forces, but can be seen as a general description of all that Jesus was doing. According to Mark he himself speaks of his ministry in these terms, 'No-one can enter a strong man's house and carry off his possessions unless he first ties up the strong man. Then he can rob his house' (Mark 3:27).

The witness of the New Testament insists, on the one hand, on the actuality of these destructive spiritual powers against which, in his deliverances and supremely on his cross, Jesus fights his battle and wins his victory. On the other hand it refuses to bring them out of the shadows and into the limelight. It acknowledges the opposition of evil but refuses to be specific about its nature. It speaks unspecifically and mysteriously of principalities and powers, of the prince of this world, the powers of this dark world, of the devil and Satan, but the only thing that matters about them is that Christ has broken and overcome them. To be very interested in anything else about them is to pay them a compliment they do not deserve and dangerously to divert our attention from the one who has dealt with them and can save us from them.

That biblical reticence extends to the question whether these evil forces are personal or impersonal. Sometimes Paul, as we have seen, speaks of Christ's defeated foes in personal terms, Satan, devil, prince of darkness, but sometimes in impersonal terms as sin, death and even the law. Both sets of terms represent different aspects of our experience of evil. Sometimes we seem to be assailed by a deliberate, planned campaign of an intelligent malevolence that knows where we are most vulnerable and attacks us at the worst places at the worst time. At other times we seem to be set upon by a destructive uncaring fate that is blind to our situation and deaf to our pleas and that uncaringly frustrates our relationship with God and our desires to please him. So Paul can in Romans 7 see himself as 'a prisoner of the law of sin at work within my members' (v. 23), from which he cannot free himself but has to look for help beyond himself in what Christ has done.

If we get involved in inevitably inconclusive arguments about whether evil is personal or impersonal, we can easily miss the main point; Christ in his life and his death encounters not just the moral failings and wrongdoing of individual people, but great cosmic forces of evil that have gained a grip on every part of the world's life. These forces can be shadowy background factors involved in physical disease, mental derangement, moral iniquity on the personal level, and on the social level in societies and cultures that are constructed on foundations that make it hard for people to hear and understand what God is saying to them, in tyrannies that unjustly oppress people and deprive them of the kind of life that God means them to have, in natural disasters of all kinds and in many other ways.

On the personal level we are all from time to time aware of being trapped in habits, desires and obsessions that we recognise as evil and yet from which we cannot by effort and resolve free ourselves. In late twentieth century Britain we are all, Christians included, influenced and to some extent driven by social forces and values that are far from friendly to our gospel and that make it harder rather than easier for us and for those we want to reach in our evangelism to understand and follow Christ's word. It is in these realms, rather than in bizarre occult manifestations, that we are liable to encounter the principalities and powers of which the New Testament speaks.

In such encounters we need to beware of the curiosity and even the anxiety that could draw us into the shadows where these malign forces are lurking and where they wield their power. We are neither to fight them nor fear them, because the battle against them has already been fought and won by Jesus on the cross. We are to have dealings not with them but with him; we do not need to win victories of our own, but only to share in his victory that is already accomplished and we can have confidence that, although these powers may harry and oppress us, in our relationship with Christ we can be led through that oppression to the triumph. Our faith in Christ assures us that what the principalities and powers devised for our destruction, Christ can use for our redemption, just as he made what they did to him the stepping stones that led to his rising and his rule at God's right hand.

We have looked at the nature of the enemy, but now we have to look at the nature of the victory. In the Second World War the allies knew they had won only when Berlin had fallen, when the enemy had thrown against them everything he had and the central heartlands of his evil empire had been penetrated and overthrown. There were other battles and other victories along the long road to Berlin, but the battle that consummated the victory was fought there, street by street and house by house till the whole place was occupied.

So with Jesus; the outposts of the satanic empire were attacked and overwhelmed in the villages of Galilee, but, before evil could be finally defeated, he had to meet the whole force of its legions and penetrate right into the destructive heart of its purposes and power. This he did on Calvary. John Calvin expounded the phrase of the Apostles' Creed, 'He descended into hell' as describing not some underworld journey that Jesus took after his death but rather the deadly depths of his suffering on the cross. All hell was there that day in the excruciating pain that the Lord suffered, in his rejection by his people and his desertion by his disciples, in the black spiritual abandonment that made him cry out, 'My God, my God, why have you forsaken me?' (Mark 15:34). Here the whole mystery of evil hurtled itself against him through its human agents. Sin, death and hell fell upon him in consuming fury. There was no weapon in his armoury that Satan did not deploy against the Son of God.

All hell was there that day on Calvary, and therefore all hell was defeated that day on Calvary when the man on the cross, despite the very worst that the devil and his legions could do to him, rose from the dead. His resurrection is the first-fruit of his victory, the certifying sign that the victim has conquered, the oppressed has subdued his oppressors, what was in him was mightier than what was in them. The last word is not with evil but with goodness, not with hell but with heaven, not with death but with life. The resurrection is the sign of his victory; without it we could not know that he had conquered and would be left in holy Saturday despair. The fruits of victory begin to be gathered on Easter morning, but the battle is fought and the victory is won on the cross.

But what was it in Jesus that was mightier than what was in his enemies? This is where our military metaphors have to be handled with great care. What happens on Calvary is indeed a battle fought at great cost to glorious victory, but it is a battle of a very peculiar kind that needs to be understood in its own terms. This is not a battle in which the side that has the biggest battalions prevails, where superior supernatural power wins the day, where God crushes his opponents by the sheer weight of his divine might.

The charismatic renewal in our own day has very rightly reminded us of the power of the gospel, but we need to be very careful about what kind of power we are talking about. Jesus did not smash his opponents by the dramatic exercise of divine energy that some Charismatics seem to be looking for. As he approached the cross he specifically rejected that route to victory when he said to his disciples, 'Put your sword back in its place ... for all who draw the sword will die by the sword. Do you think I cannot call on my Father, and he will at once put at my disposal more than twelve legions of angels. But how then would the Scriptures be fulfilled that say it must happen in this way?' (Matthew 26:52–4). To attack the enemy in that violent way, whether the violence be natural or supernatural, would be to fight him with his own weapons and so play into his hands and Jesus knows that there is no ultimate victory to be won with such weapons and in such a way. So he strips himself of all the protections that his divinity might afford and engages in the battle with nothing but the vulnerability of his self-giving love.

It is that love that wins the day. The passiontide hymn, 'O come and mourn with me awhile' by F. W. Faber, gets it exactly right,

> 'O love of God! O sin of man!
> In this dread act your strength is tried
> and victory remains with love,
> Jesus, our Lord is crucified!'

The only thing that could defeat evil is Calvary love. Force may be needed to contain some of its outward manifestations in the short term, but evil yields only to Calvary love. The love that gives itself without reserve to God on behalf of the world is proved on the cross to be strong enough and tough enough to put all the legions of hell who have thrown all their forces against it totally to flight. Hell is conquered, sin is forgiven and its power broken, death is taken captive and made the way to new life when Jesus in love gives himself for us on the cross.

Love is almighty because God *is* love. He lives his own life in love, in the self-giving of the Father to the Son and the Son to the Father in the Holy Spirit. To share and reflect that love he makes the world and men and women to be the mirrors of his love. When his world rejects his love and falls into the hands of his foes, he expels them and repossesses what is his own by the great act of love that begins at Christmas and culminates on the cross.

The victorious power of that love is the heart of the mystery of Christ's death and resurrection. The consequence of that for us is that we shall share that victory as we yield to that love. The crucified Christ offers us no immunity from enemy attack and all the suffering it can involve, but he promises that we shall find his love in the midst of it all and see over and over again the signs of his victory breaking out in our lives on the small scale just as it broke out on the large scale when he rose from the dead.

If we want healing, then we have to seek his love because it is in communities in which his love prevails that authentic healing happens. If we want deliverance from sin, we have to ask to be possessed afresh by the love of Jesus because it is in what has been called the expulsive power of a new affection for him that the old habits and attitudes are broken and we are made more like him. If we seek justice in society it will be won not by violence and denunciation but by the tough love that confronts oppressors and the gentle love that cares for the oppressed. If we want renewal in the Church, then we must ask that the love of God should be poured into our hearts through the Holy Spirit that he has given us from the cross (Romans 5:5). All the charismatic gifts and dramatic manifestations of the Spirit are useless and destructive if they are not used in the service of love, as Paul makes clear in 1 Corinthians 13.

These are in outline some of the consequences that follow from the kind of victory that Jesus won on Calvary, a battle royal indeed, but a battle different from all other warfare, because it was waged by God's incarnate love for love of God's people and God's world to give them victory over their foes. 'Thanks be to God who goes on giving us the victory through our Lord Jesus Christ' (1 Corinthians 15:57).

POINTS TO PONDER

- What do you understand by the 'principalities and powers' that Christ conquered on the cross?

- Does the cross make us all pacifists? Has the use of force alongside the self-giving of love any part to play in the restraining and overcoming of evil?

- If, as Christians claim, Christ has decisively conquered evil on the cross, why is it still so powerful in the world today?

8

Participation

At this window we are standing right at the point where the modern and ancient wings of the house make contact again with each other. From the first days of the Church until now Christians have known that the cross of Jesus has implications not just for his life but for theirs and that the cross that he carries, although it is unique to him, requires that we ourselves also should be involved in cross-carrying operations that are in many respects the same shape as his own.

His word to his first disciples makes that quite clear. In Mark 8 Jesus announces for the first time that 'the Son of man must suffer many things and be rejected by the elders, chief priests and teachers of the law and that he must be killed' (8:31). When a bewildered and affronted Peter protests that this cannot be so and tries to dissuade him, Jesus not only rebukes Peter for rejecting the cross for his master, but goes on to tell him and all who join him in the disciple company that he and they will face their own crosses as well, as an essential component and inevitable consequence of their discipleship: 'If anyone would come after me, he must deny himself and take up his cross and follow me. For whoever wants to save his life will lose it, but whoever loses his life for me and for the gospel will save it' (8:34–5). We shall see more of what this means later, but notice for the moment that what we are to carry is our own cross, not that of Jesus. This implies a distinction between the two, and yet to speak of Christian self-denial and sacrifice of life in terms of carrying a cross underlines the close and integral connection between what happened to Jesus on Calvary and what is going to happen to us as we follow him.

Theologians down the centuries have made a distinction that goes back to the New Testament between what Jesus did *for us* once for all on Calvary and what he now does *in and through us* by his Spirit as a result of Calvary. What he did *for us* there is his work and achievement alone and we had no part in the doing of it. On his cross he suffers and dies, lifted up alone.

The Gospel writers emphasise that fact in their different ways. Mark and Matthew tell us that, when Judas betrayed Jesus in Gethsemane, 'Then all the disciples deserted him and fled' (Matthew 26:56, Mark 14:50). The only part they can then play in the ongoing Passion story is for Peter to deny three times with curses that he ever had anything to do with Jesus. John deals with the disciples more gently, 'Near the cross of Jesus stood his mother, his mother's sister, Mary the wife of Clopas, and Mary Magdalene ... and the disciple whom he [Jesus] loved' (19:25–6). Where faith has failed, love still keeps watch, but their presence simply underlines their helplessness. They can sorrow over him and sympathise with his pain, but they have at that moment no understanding of or part in what he has been doing there. Our salvation depends not upon them but upon him alone; it is his lips only that can utter the great cry of dying victory, '*Tetelestai*', 'it is accomplished'.

That so much needs to be emphasised today and that is why in this book I have been trying to emphasise it. The cross of Jesus is not just an example of love for us to follow, it is a gift of salvation for us to receive and it can only be received from his hands. It is he alone who has reconciled us to God, he alone who has offered the pure and acceptable sacrifice that we failed to offer, he alone who did what needed to be done to bring us back into right relationship to God, he alone in whom God came to share our suffering, he alone who won the victory over the principalities and powers of darkness and so he alone who arose from the dead. That needs to be said and it cannot be said too often, because it is part of our sin to believe that we can make at least some contribution to saving ourselves from our sin. We need constant reminders that, as Toplady put it in his great hymn 'Rock of ages, cleft for me',

> Not the labours of my hands
> Can fulfil Thy law's demands:
> Could my zeal no respite know,
> could my tears for ever flow,
> all for sin could not atone,
> *Thou must save and Thou alone.*

The windows that we have been looking through till now have, I hope, helped to show us different aspects of what he alone could do and has in fact done for us on the cross.

But having done it without us, he enables us to follow him in the same path. A pioneer making a road through a wild countryside has obstacles to deal with that subsequent drivers along that road will never face and needs equipment to deal with them that is far beyond the ken and the competence of those who come after. Nevertheless the whole point of making the road is that these others should be able to make the same journey and reach the same destination. So it is with the way of the cross: it is constructed by Jesus at a cost that he alone must pay and we cannot travel that way till he has made it. Yet the way is made precisely in order that we may travel it, that we may make the journey back to God along it. To travel

94

along it, we need the kind of self-denial and self-giving that is appropriate to the first pioneer of our salvation.

In John's Gospel, when Peter, in response to Jesus' talk about his approaching death, says that he will lay down his life for him, Jesus does not rebuke him for making a promise that he has not the courage to keep, but says to him that the time is not yet ripe for such an offer, 'Where I am going you cannot follow now, but you will follow later' (13:36). Before Peter can give his life for Jesus, Jesus has to give his life for Peter. Before Jesus has died for him, Peter, relying on his own resources, can only deny him, but after Jesus has died and risen, Peter can follow him along the same road to his own death and resurrection.

That then is the subject of this chapter – what it means for us to participate in the cross of Christ after he has borne it for us. This window is, as it were, the top half of a door. Here we do not just look at what he has done for us without our help, but we join the action, we follow the crucified along his road.

He is ahead of us on that road, so that what happened to him on it is a clue to what will happen to us as we follow him, and the way he dealt with what happened to him becomes his command to us that we should behave in the same way. Dietrich Bonhoeffer, in his classic book *The Cost of Discipleship*, made a famous distinction between what he called cheap grace and costly grace. Cheap grace is to seek to benefit from what Christ did on the cross without being willing to follow in the way of the crucified; it is to expect forgiveness without repentance, free acceptance by God without changing our lifestyle to conform to the commands of God, turning the good news of 'Just as I am, I come' into the presumptuous complacency of 'Just as I am I stay', a passport to joy, healing and triumph that exempts us from pain and suffering, a moving straight on to the new life of Easter and the power and excitement of Pentecost without on the way having to come to terms with the cross as the place from which Jesus calls us to share in his sufferings.

Cheap grace comes in many forms, it can be indulged in by only partially committed Christians who want God to serve them without having any intention of serving him. Equally it can afflict charismatic Christians who can come to expect to be miraculously and immediately delivered from all trouble, pain and suffering. Common to all its forms is a refusal to follow Christ when the road leads to the cross.

Costly grace might seem at first sight to be a contradiction in terms, since the very word grace speaks of a free gift that is given to all who will receive it and that can never be bought or earned. Such indeed is the grace of Christ that all through his ministry from first to last it was offered to all who would receive it, and especially to people like Zacchaeus, Mary Magdalene, the woman taken in adultery who were completely undeserving of it. It was grace because it was given for nothing, but it was costly because it demanded everything of those who received it. To receive grace is to relate to Jesus and to relate to Jesus can only mean to follow him on the way that leads to the cross.

The costliness of the relationship, far from detracting from its graciousness, enhances it, because for Christians the way of the cross is a way that leads to the new life of the resurrection, and closeness to Christ can be at its most real and most intimate when he and we are sharers in suffering. He is indeed with us when we are led by green pastures and still waters, but there is a new dimension to our relationship with him when we walk through the valley of the shadow of death and discover that his rod and his staff, his attentive, protecting companionship, comfort us there when most other forms of comfort are gone.

One of the deep encouragements of pastoral ministry over the years has been to come into contact with people who have been going through terrible ordeals that silenced any words of comfort I might have spoken and that could easily have made faith falter and fail, and to discover that in the darkness they had discovered the Jesus of the scars and were bound to him in a way they had never been when things were going well. No wonder that Paul, in prison in Rome, should write to his friends in Philippi about the consuming ambition of his life in these terms, 'I want to know Christ and the power of his resurrection and *the fellowship of sharing in his sufferings, becoming like him in his death*, and so, somehow, to attain to the resurrection from the dead' (Philippians 3:10–11, italics mine). The road that Paul is walking is the road that leads via Calvary and, because he has found it a good road to the best of all destinations, he records here his resolve and desire to walk it to the end.

If we try to identify a little what it means to take up our cross and follow Christ, there are three factors that we can specify; the first is self-denial. Taking up your cross means denying yourself, not because a regime of stern self-discipline is necessarily a good thing in itself, but because deliverance from a controlling and inordinate self-concern and self-indulgence is a prerequisite for being able to give yourself to God and to other people.

If the essence of sin is self-concern at the expense of concern with God and the needs of others, then salvation from sin must involve an escape from that self-concern into an ability to give yourself to God and to others without counting the cost. It was in these terms that Jesus spoke of what he was about to do on the cross: 'unless a grain of wheat falls to the ground and dies, it remains only a single seed. But if it dies, it produces many seeds. The man who loves his life will lose it, while the man who hates his life in this world will keep it for eternal life' (John 12:24–5). A life whose purpose is self-fulfilment will at the end of the day be an unfulfilled life, but a life that is given to God and to others will be fruitful for God and for others and will find in the giving away of life a new dimension of fulfilled living for itself.

That is on the one hand Jesus' understanding of what he is himself about to do in his death, but it is also a rule of life for his disciples as well, as the next verse makes clear, 'Whoever serves me must follow me; and where I am, my servant also will be' (12:26). To follow him means to walk the road of disciplined self-denial after him. It is in that context that the traditional Lenten disciplines are to be understood and their value assessed. In what measure do they make us masters of ourselves and so free to follow Christ on the road of self-giving to the cross?

The cross we carry is not however confined to the disciplines we impose on ourselves, it involves also the persecution and the various kinds of opposition that others impose on us. It is sheer romanticism to suppose that, when the kind of love that Jesus showed appears in our kind of world in all its fallenness, making the kind of claims that Jesus made for it, it will be welcomed and accepted on every side. The Gospel evidence is that, to the contrary, it will be crucified, both by the action taken against it by those, like the Jewish priests and Roman authorities, whose lifestyle and power structures it threatens but also by the complicity of those who, like the deserting disciples, are attracted by it but are not ready to take the consequences of identifying themselves with it. If Winston Churchill, when he assumed office in 1940, could offer the nation only blood, sweat, toil and tears, Jesus offers his disciples no easier way. If we follow him it must not be with any expectation of a cushioned rise to glory, but because we have found in him, as the nation at that time found in Churchill, a man who can be trusted because he reckons with all the dark realities but has in himself the authority and the resources that will lead us through it all to victory, and will always be in charge at every dangerous and painful step of the way.

The New Testament writers keep on emphasising that we are not to be surprised when the gospel proclaimed and lived rouses up fierce opposition against itself. Jesus said it would be so,

> If the world hates you, keep in mind that it hated me first. If you belonged to the world, it would love you as its own. As it is, you do not belong to the world, but I have chosen you out of the world. That is why the world hates you. Remember the words I spoke to you: 'No servant is greater than his master.' If they persecuted me, they will persecute you also. (John 15:18–20)

That persecution can take many subtle forms besides the exercise of crude physical violence, although Christians still have to endure that for their faith in many parts of the world today. Alongside that however there is what we might call intellectual persecution, the kind of thing that Paul encountered at Athens and described in his letter to the Corinthians. The message of the resurrection of Jesus was so alien to the Athenian philosophers that they responded to it with sneers (Acts 17:32), and the message of the cross again and again proved itself to be 'foolishness to the Greeks' as well as being 'a stumbling block to Jews' (1 Corinthians 1:23).

We also have to live in a world whose basic belief system is quite unfriendly to the gospel so that those who profess it are seen as irrational and weird, and where the things the gospel stands for are regarded as having little public relevance but only the strange private views of an out of touch minority. This hurts, not just because of the rejection, but because we also are people of our day and the clash inside ourselves of the gospel we believe and the ruling philosophies of the world often produces periods of very painful doubt and confusion. To struggle with these is part of the cost of following Jesus in our day, as it has always been.

There is also what we might call the ethical persecution that taking a stand for the gospel and its values will bring to us in a society that has increasingly fewer values of its own except self-promotion and self-fulfilment. Christian believers who refuse to make a secret of their faith and try to follow its implications, positive and negative, in the lives they live among people every day will often find themselves estranged from their friends and even their families as a result, denied advancement at work, subjected to subtle or not so subtle ridicule and ostracism in their social relationships, and faced with all kinds of clashes of loyalty where faithfulness to Christ will involve a refusal to follow the practices and expectations of those for whom they have a regard or on whose favour they depend. In such situations craven compromises are a real temptation; to be faithful hurts, but such hurts are part of the cost of following Christ on the way to the cross.

To carry the cross on its negative side is both to practise self-denial and to endure persecution, but on its positive side it is to follow Jesus in the self-giving love for God and for people that is at the heart of Calvary and that gives it its atoning power. That self-giving love shines forth in its full glory when it is not just love for friends, but love for enemies as well, as it was on the cross. Jesus has a right to exhort us to 'love your enemies and pray for those that persecute you', (Matthew 5:44) because that is precisely what he himself did on Calvary when he prayed, 'Father, forgive them for they do not know what they are doing' (Luke 23:34). The way he treated those who opposed him is the rule for our treatment of those who, in some of the ways we have just been describing, actively oppose us. Peter in his letter makes the point clearly, '. . . Christ suffered for you, leaving you an example that you should follow in his steps. "He committed no sin and no deceit was found in his mouth." When they hurled their insults at him, he did not retaliate; when he suffered he made no threats. Instead he entrusted himself to him who judges justly' (1 Peter 2:21–3). Christians are to be blotting paper not boomerangs for evil, they are to mop it up rather than to rebound it back, and positively they are not simply to endure evil passively and non-violently but they are to show those who do evil to them the only thing that can undo the evil and change its perpetrators – the tough and soon to conquer love that Jesus showed on the cross to us all.

This has all kinds of imploctions both personal and social for the way a Christian man or woman and a Christian society deal with those who oppose, undermine and attempt to destroy them, whether by physical violence or in more subtle ways. The cross shows us how Christ treated his enemies and that must be binding for the way we treat ours. There is the closest possible connection between the two as the Lord's Prayer makes clear, 'Forgive us our sins as we forgive those who sin against us.'

Its implications however extend far beyond the realm of personal relationships; they are, for example, highly relevant to the contemporary debate about society's reactions to crime and those who commit it. Prisons and police personnel are necessary if crime and criminals are to be restrained, but if the perpetrators of crime are to be transformed and changed, that will be achieved neither by harsh nor yet by indulgent regimes in courts and prisons, but in finding ways to reflect to them the penetrating judgement and the inexhaustible hope that come from the tough love that Jesus showed on the cross. It was to such a perpetrator of evil against society that Jesus from the cross said, 'Today you will be with me in paradise' (Luke 23:43).

The calling of the Christian is to follow Christ on the road of self-denial, of bearing persecution and of responding to evil with his kind of forgiving self-giving. In all this he is our example, but if he is only our example, he will also be our despair. If all we can do is look through a window that shows us what he was like on Calvary and that exhorts us to be like that every day, the more we try, the more impossible we shall find it and the more dismally we shall fail. We shall not be able to walk the way of the cross unless we first share in the grace of the cross. A Jesus who is only an example is too exterior to us and remote from us to give us the help that we need to follow in his steps.

We need therefore to turn to that rich vein of New Testament teaching that tells us that the crucified Jesus offers us not just a demanding ethic to obey but a poured out life to share. He does not just give himself *for* us but he gives himself *to* us, and the second follows from the first. That is made clear in the Eucharist where Jesus bids us, 'Take, eat, this is my body which is given for you.' What he gives to God on the cross on our behalf – and that is nothing less than his body, his very self – is also to penetrate right into the heart of our bodies, our very selves, so that everything that he shows us in his death, he also gives to us as the provision by which we shall be able to become like him and walk in his way.

That is what Paul is describing in terms of vivid personal experience in Galatians 2:20: 'I have been crucified with

Christ and I no longer live, but Christ lives in me. The life I live in the body, I live by faith in the Son of God, who loved me and gave himself for me.' Paul is not talking here about the elimination of his personhood, but rather the elimination of his isolation and independence of God and his grace. It is that independent self-sufficient 'I' who has been crucified with Christ and who no longer lives; he has been replaced by the new 'I' who is so open to Christ in faith that Christ and everything he has to give are now at the very centre of his being, so that the disciplined, suffering and life-giving love of Christ now surges through his being and has started radically to reshape his attitudes and his actions.

In his teaching in Romans 6 Paul interprets our baptism as our radical identification with and participation in Christ in his death and resurrection: 'Don't you know that all of us who were baptised in Christ Jesus were baptised into his death? We were therefore buried with him through baptism into death in order that, just as Christ was raised from the dead through the glory of the Father, we too may live a new life' (6:3–4). What this means for our actual Christian living is expounded in the rest of the chapter but may be summed up in verses 10 and 11, 'The death he died, he died to sin once for all; but the life he lives, he lives to God. In the same way count yourselves dead to sin but alive to God in Christ Jesus.'

On Calvary, in some of the ways we have been describing in our previous chapters, Christ 'died to sin'; by bearing the worst that human sin and the evil powers lurking behind it could do to him, he broke its hold upon him. His tough love won its life-giving victory over everything that stood against it. Paul is saying here that what Christ did out there on Calvary, he is able to do in here at the heart of our own lives so that the evil things that lurk inside us, that skew our thinking, dominate our wills and control our actions, can have their power over us broken. We can die to them so that they cannot get us any more and the controlling factor in our lives and their activities can be the very same conquering, reconciling, liberating, self-sacrificing love that Jesus showed on Calvary. It need not stay out there in him; when we trust him and stay close to him it will show itself in here in us.

If we turn away from him, if the faith connection between us is loosened and broken, then sin is all ready to take over again, as we well know. Only in him is it conquered, only in him does sin die and life reign, but to be in him, to be constantly nourished by what he is and has to give, to go on daily eating his flesh and drinking his blood, so that his life may be in us – that is how we stop gazing wistfully through a window at a cross in history and become aware in our own experience of the death to sin and the new life with God that are ours in him.

POINTS TO PONDER

- 'The cross of Jesus is not just an example of love for us to follow; it is a gift of salvation for us to receive and it can be received only from his hands.' What do you make of this?

- Does modern Christianity as practised in our churches often offer 'cheap' rather than 'costly' grace?

- How in personal and practical terms do you understand what it would mean for you to take up your cross and follow Jesus?

9

Glory

We have completed our present circuit of the windows
on the cross. We have not looked through every window
but have in fact confined ourselves to some of the main
scriptural and modern viewpoints on the cross so that
there is a large historical wing of the Christian house
that we have not visited at all. There we could look at
Calvary through the eyes of those who have gone before
us in the faith, the ancient fathers of the Church in East
and West, the medieval schoolmen, the sixteenth-century
reformers, the evangelical and catholic theologians of the
centuries immediately before our own. All of them in
their day and in their way have looked at the crucified
and risen Saviour from where they stood in history and
have seen things from which we can still learn and profit
greatly.

There are many windows, and no doubt there will be
many more for as long as the Church continues and its
members go on grappling with the heart of the gospel.
Many windows, but all of them seeking to survey the one
cross and confirming and correcting one another, so that
ideally we need to look through them all. In this short
study we have concentrated on the scriptural windows
because they come first, offer close-up views and take us
nearer the cross than anything that comes after. To these
we have added two of the more modern windows that
show us features of the gospel of the cross that are already

present in the Scriptures but have been highlighted in our own day because they are more easily accessible to our contemporaries and to ourselves.

In this final chapter we are not going to look at yet another window but rather think about the light that shines through them all. The name of that light is glory: 'God, who said, "Let light shine out of darkness," made his light shine in our hearts to give us the light of the knowledge of the glory of God in the face of Christ' (2 Corinthians 4:6). Light and glory go together and they both stream forth from the face of Jesus Christ, surmounted as it was once by a crown of thorns on Calvary and now with a crown of kingly authority at the right hand of God.

That the second crown is glorious is immediately obvious, but the New Testament insists that the glory has its source at the cross. It is indeed true that the deed done on Calvary takes place in deep darkness, so that, according to the Gospels, even the sun refused to shine on it. All the lights are out till they are switched on again on Easter morning. Nevertheless, when they are switched on, it soon becomes quite clear that the source of their shining, the unlikely location from which God makes the light of life shine again from the midst of the darkness, is the glorious man on the shameful cross.

Till the lights are switched on at the resurrection we cannot see his glory; no divine brightness shines from Calvary, the cross of Jesus is but another sad martyrdom, the undeserved victimisation of one more good man who was weak by evil people who were strong, one more to add to the countless number that shame and disfigure our history. Here perhaps a final brave flickering of human goodness, but certainly no sign of a glorious sunrise of divine grace.

But if this man is raised from the dead, then the uniqueness of his rising highlights the uniqueness of his cross and singles it out from all the other crosses of all the other victims on all the other hills that ever were. When the light is switched on at the resurrection we see glory where before we could see only shame and the light of the glory of God shines from the thorn-crowned face of Jesus. Without the resurrection we could not see his glory, but when we do see it, we realise that it is the glory of his cross.

As Professor Morna Hooker puts it in a less figurative way, 'The death and resurrection of Jesus must be seen together: his death is meaningless until God gives it meaning by raising him to life. Even when the resurrection is not specifically mentioned, it is assumed.'* In this book the resurrection has not often been specifically mentioned, but it has been assumed on every page; all the windows we have looked through would be dark and unrevealing if the rising of Jesus had not switched on the light in which we could see the many facets of the glory of the cross.

A few paragraphs further on Professor Hooker continues,

> The idea – common to Paul and John – that God's glory is revealed in the death of Christ is perhaps the New Testament's most profound insight into its meaning. For the background of the Greek word for glory (*doxa*) is the Hebrew *kabod* a word which is used to express what God is. The belief that God is revealed in the shame and weakness of the cross is a profound insight into the nature of God.

In John's Gospel, in place of the Gethsemane story that

---

* *Not Ashamed of the Gospel* (Carlisle, The Paternoster Press, 1994), p. 139.

the other three tell, the passion of Jesus is introduced by an alternative account of Jesus' prayer to the Father about his approaching death, ' "Now my heart is troubled and what shall I say? Father, save me from this hour? No, it was for this very reason I came to this hour. Father, glorify your name!" Then a voice came from heaven, "I have glorified it and will glorify it again" ' (12:27–8). The cross is to be the supreme revelation of the Father's glory; there we shall see in his Son what he is like and what he is willing to do for us and find that it is glorious through and through.

So Paul in 1 Corinthians, referring to the hostile and mysterious principalities and powers that were the ultimate perpetrators of Calvary says, 'None of the rulers of this age understood it [God's secret wisdom], for if they had, they would not have crucified the Lord of glory' (2:8). The cross was a hideous miscalculation on the part of the powers of darkness, because if you pierce and wound the one who is the Lord of glory, what comes out through his wounds are the rivers of his glory, the liberating, forgiving, sacrificing, life-giving and victorious grace that we have been describing in these chapters and that all have their focus and their locus in the cross.

In similar vein Paul exclaims to the Galatians who were being invited to glory in all sorts of other things, 'God forbid that I should glory except in the cross of the Lord Jesus Christ, through which the world has been crucified to me, and I to the world' (Galatians 6:14). The Greek verb that the older versions translate 'glory' in this passage can best be rendered 'boast'. The basic meaning is that Paul is boasting about, glorying in, the very thing into which God has compacted and through which he has expressed the glory of his own nature and love towards us. Paul is thankfully rejoicing in all the Godhead that God has put into the crucified Jesus.

When something is bruised and wounded, then what is in it pours out of it. When an orange is opened, squeezed, and under pressure then for the first time we become aware of what lies under the skin and can taste whether the juice is bitter or sweet. So with us: it is often in the pressure and trauma of suffering that we show what is under the surface, whether at the heart of us we are sweet or bitter, believing or unbelieving, filled with fear or filled with faith.

John is thinking in that sort of way about Jesus when he tells us what happened when he had uttered his great cry of triumph, bowed his head and died. 'One of the soldiers pierced Jesus' side with a spear, bringing a sudden flow of blood and water' (19:34). This is so important for John that in the next verse he goes on to underline it, 'The man who saw it has given testimony, and his testimony is true. He knows that he tells the truth and he testifies so that you also may believe.' In his prologue to the Gospel John says that the story he is about to tell is about God's living, personal Word who became flesh in Jesus and continues, 'We have seen his glory, the glory of the One and Only, who came from the Father, full of grace and truth' (1:14). At the start of the story we are told that his glory consists of the grace and truth of which he was full and at the end of the story, when the work of the cross is completed, we are told that the soldier's spear released that of which he was full; the glory of God that was grace and truth came pouring out in the form of blood and water.

The cross of Jesus is glorious with the very glory of God himself and shows us that his glory is not in his surpassing greatness above us or his sovereign power over us, but in his self-giving love towards us. That love is gracious because it does not rest upon our goodness or our deserving; it is true to us even when we are anything but true to him, and in that way is full of grace and truth.

That glorious grace and truth reach us from Calvary as blood and water from Christ's wounded side. In the New Testament blood stands for the forgiveness of yesterday and water stands for new life for today and John is telling us that both come to us from the cross. 'Freedom from sin through his blood' is a phrase that in one form or another is at the very heart of what the New Testament has to say about the results of Christ's death, most notably in his own words over the cup at the Last Supper: 'This is my blood of the new covenant, which is poured out for many for the forgiveness of sins' (Matthew 26:28). It is important that we should not allow any modern squeamishness about blood to obscure the point that the self-sacrifice of Jesus, in ways which we have been looking at in previous chapters, is the means by which God rescues us from the sinful past and brings us back into right relationship to himself again – and that is glory.

When some years ago I went to Jerusalem, my room was on the top floor of a Franciscan guest-house; it gave on to a flat roof that overlooked the Via Dolorosa, the long street that Jesus walked on the way to his crucifixion. My first night there it was stiflingly hot and the cocks seemed never to stop crowing, so that I got little sleep. Towards dawn I wandered to the edge of the balconied roof and looked at the nearly empty street below. It was not entirely empty because half-way along it was a donkey pulling a dustbin into which was being loaded all the refuse of the previous day. The street where the donkey had not yet reached was full of the rubbish of yesterday but, where the donkey with the dustbin had passed, everything was clean and clear ready for the new day. A donkey with a dustbin, it makes you think of the foolishness of the cross and the abasement of the one who walked that

110

same road on the same kind of enterprise, 'Behold the Lamb of God who takes away the rubbish of the world.'

His abasement is also his glory that, for love of us, not only washed his disciples' feet in the upper room, but gave himself so that his poured out love might wash clean our tarnished humanity. In the virtue of his cross he still walks the roads of the world, so that everything that was dirty before he came to it is made clean as he passes by. It is the twofold cleanness that Toplady celebrates in his hymn, 'Be of sin the double cure; Cleanse me from its guilt and power.'

The cleansing from guilt is immediate and total; when in faith we approach God, not in virtue of any good deed we have done or any fine quality that we possess but with our whole trust in Christ and his sacrifice, all that before stood between us and God is immediately removed and our right relationship to God as the loved and accepted children of the Father is restored. By Christ and in Christ the wrongness of our fallen humanity goes to death and is replaced by the new humanity that is acceptable to God, because it reflects back to him his own love for us and for all.

The glory of the gospel is that our forgiveness and acceptance with God is not a long process with an uncertain outcome, so that we cannot know where we stand with him till it is all completed and the books are opened on the Last Day. Our acceptance does not depend on something that has still to be done by us, but on that which has already been done completely and for ever on our behalf by Jesus on the cross.

To put the same thing another way, our forgiveness and acceptance are not prizes to be won but gifts to be received. As the letter to the Ephesians puts it, 'In him we *have* redemption through his blood, the forgiveness of sins, in accordance with the riches of God's grace that he lavished on us with all wisdom and understanding' (1:7–8, italics mine). Notice the present use – we *have* redemption – and we know that we have it, because it has been given to us as a result of what Christ did on the cross. Our faith is the empty hand that we stretch out to receive this gift, 'By grace you have been saved, through faith – and this not from yourselves, it is the gift of God – not by works, so that no-one can boast. For we are God's workmanship, created in Christ Jesus to do good works, which God prepared in advance for us to do' (Ephesians 2:8–10).

Through what Christ has done our positive relationship with God has been restored. Christ crucified and risen is the line of communication that has been opened between him and us. He is, so to speak, plugged into the heart of God at one end and, on the cross, has been plugged into the depth of human misery and rebellion at the other. He is both the Son of the Father and the friend of the sinners, and through him all that the Father has for us flows to us to make us new.

As soon as we receive in faith what Christ offers, the guilt of sin is broken by his gift of forgiveness and the process of our remaking can begin. It is not that he accepts us after we have been remade to his satisfaction but rather that he accepts us as we are and then, within the security and confidence that his accepting love gives us, he begins the long process of – to speak negatively – breaking sin's power over us and – to speak positively – pouring his own life into us. First comes the acceptance and then the remaking, and not the other way round.

> Just as I am – and waiting not
> To rid my soul of one dark blot,
> To Thee, whose blood can cleanse each spot,
>   O Lamb of God, I come.

Just as I am – Thou wilt receive,
Wilt welcome, pardon, cleanse, relieve:
Because Thy promise I believe,
   O Lamb of God, I come.

(Charlotte Elliott)

This is indeed the crowning manifestation of his crucified glory, that to the weakest and the worst of us, he says, the moment that we come to him, 'Son, daughter, your sins are forgiven.'

However, as we have said already, 'Just as I am, I come' does not by any means imply, 'Just as I am, I stay'. Jesus once compared himself to the good doctor who is at the disposal of all who need him, and the worse they are, the more urgently will he attend to them. First doctors receive patients but then they go on to treat and cure them. When God in Christ has received us quite unconditionally into a loving relationship with himself, the same love sets about breaking the hold of sin upon us and making us all that he has always intended us to be.

The establishment of the relationship is immediate when we turn in faith to Christ, but the breaking of the hold of sin upon us is, as sad experience has shown most of us, the long struggle of a whole lifetime. We shall be freed from the guilt of sin long before we have been cleansed of its power. But the cross in which Christ won acceptance and forgiveness *for* us is also the means by which he will achieve deliverance from sin *in* us.

Here again we have to go back to our starting-point and emphasise that as sinners are accepted, so sin is conquered by the blood of Jesus. Here also we are bid to drink of the new covenant in his blood which is shed for many to release us from sin. Here we have to see that blood shed means life poured out, but life poured out means death. We have to reckon with the alarming fact that the cross of Jesus is both life-giving and death-dealing, and you can only share the life he gives if you will also die the death he dies.

We are back at the point we reached at the end of the last chapter when we saw how in Romans 6 Paul teaches that Christ died to sin and that in our baptism we came to share in that death. At Calvary he died, and when you die the things that have been attacking you cannot reach you any more. When he died, Caiaphas, Pilate and all the powers of darkness ranged behind him had shot their bolt, they had done their worst. As with him, so with us; you are free from sin only when you are dead, but, despair not, as far as sin is concerned, you can start dying right now. In fact you started dying when you were baptised into Christ's death and resurrection: 'For we know that our old self was crucified with him so that the body of sin might be rendered powerless, that we should no longer be slaves to sin – because anyone who has died has been freed from sin' (Romans 6:7).

In this whole passage Paul is saying that we are all engaged in a mortal conflict with sin in which one or other of the protagonists will have to die. If sin continues to conquer the ensuing death will be ours because 'the wages of sin is death' (6:23), but for Christians who are identified with Christ in his death and resurrection, the other possibility is open, that sin should die or rather that we should pass with Christ through death to a new life in which sin has no part.

This dying to sin is a painful business, just as the cross was itself supremely painful. Wrong attitudes, desires and actions are so intimately bound up with the very warp and woof of our being that, if they are exterminated, a bit of ourselves will have to die with them. That throws more light on what Paul meant when he said, 'I have been crucified with Christ' (Galatians 2:20). There was indeed triumph and relief in that, but also much pain, because it is never pleasant to be crucified – not pleasant but now possible, made possible by the cross.

Paul can be quite specific about what needs to be put to death in us, 'Put to death, therefore, whatever belongs to your earthly nature: sexual immorality, impurity, lust, evil desires and greed, which is idolatry . . . You must rid yourselves of all such things as these: anger, rage, malice, slander and filthy language from your lips' (Colossians 3:5, 8). It is a formidable list and every one of us will have to say 'That's me' about more than one item on it.

The good news is that, although these things and the part of us that connives in and enjoys these things, cannot be fundamentally changed by good intentions and moral resolutions to do better next time, they can be dealt with by the death-dealing blood of Christ, by the power of his self-giving love to make an end of the control of these things in our lives and to do it again and again, whenever they raise their ugly heads. We are not called upon to fight sin in the supposed strength of our own wills or our own goodness, but to bring it to Christ to confess it, to ask that, as he died to it, so may we in union with him, and to expect that we shall, step by step and day by day, be removed from the sphere of its power to new life in which it has no part.

The glory of the cross is that it goes on working in precisely that way. It is no theological theory but accomplished fact that Paul celebrates when he says to the Corinthians,

Do not be deceived: Neither the sexually immoral nor idolaters nor adulterers nor male prostitutes nor sodomites nor thieves nor the greedy nor drunkards nor slanderers nor swindlers will enter the kingdom of God.

115

> *And that is what some of you were. But you were*
> *washed, you were sanctified, you were justified in the*
> *name of the Lord Jesus Christ and by the Spirit of our*
> *God.* (1 Corinthians 6:9–11, italics mine)

We are not delivered from sin by the intentions we form
or the disciplines we impose, but only when we are ready
to let the death of Christ put to death everything in us
that contradicts Christ, when, in other words, we drink
his blood. This is his message: Come to the Eucharist,
come to the cross and die!

From his side comes the blood of his sacrifice in which
we are forgiven and by which we shall ultimately be set
free. But the dying is always and only for the sake of the
living, 'If we have died with Christ, we believe that we
will also live with him' (Romans 6:8). Or, in John's way
of putting it, from the side of Christ, pierced by the
soldier's spear there comes not only death-dealing blood
but life-giving water (John 19:34). In John's Gospel water
always stands for the Holy Spirit, and for John the Holy
Spirit is Jesus' supreme gift given at the cross. In John 7
we read of Jesus' visit to Jerusalem at the Jewish Feast of
Tabernacles,

> On the last and greatest day of the Feast, Jesus stood
> and said with a loud voice, 'Let anyone who is thirsty
> come to me! Let anyone who believes in me come and
> drink! As Scripture says, "From his heart shall flow
> streams of living water." ' He was speaking of the Spirit
> which those who believed in him were to receive; for
> the Spirit was not yet given, because Jesus had not yet
> been glorified. (7:37–9)

But now Jesus is glorified by being lifted up on the cross
and the sign of his glory is that the Old Testament text
just quoted has been fulfilled, because, from his heart

116

pierced by the spear, there flow out the streams of living water that he promised. The New Testament writers differ as to when and how the Spirit was delivered. For Luke it was at Pentecost, for John on Easter evening, but all are agreed that the life-giving outpouring of the Spirit is the fruit and gift of the crucified Lord.

The way to Pentecost is Calvary; the Spirit comes from the cross. The only power the Spirit has to give is the mysterious power of the cross that keeps on manifesting itself in our weakness. The only healing that the Spirit can accomplish is the healing wrought by the love that was poured out on the cross. The all-embracing charism that the Spirit gives is to share in the life that Jesus won on the cross. We shall receive the Spirit, not when we undergo prescribed rituals or share exotic experiences but when, with Mary and John, we come to the cross and let the Crucified breathe his life upon us. Let anyone who is thirsty for life and longing for the Spirit accept his invitation, come to him, look to him, believe in him and drink deep and long at the cross.

This is his glory, that from the place of shameful execution and unimaginable suffering, he breaks the guilt and power of sin and fills us with the new life of his Spirit. We have, I hope, had glimpses of that glory as we have looked through our windows at the cross. We shall see more of it as we mirror that glory in ourselves and beam it out to the world in the midst of which our house with its inner windows on the cross is set. We shall see the full unveiled glory of what it has done for the whole of humanity and the whole of creation when with 'all the living things in creation – everything that lives in heaven and on earth and under the earth, and in the sea' we sing the new song in the new heaven and the new earth, 'Worthy is the Lamb that was sacrificed to receive power, riches, wisdom, strength, honour, glory and blessing. To the One seated on the throne and to the Lamb be all praise, honour, glory and power for ever and ever' (Revelation 5:12–13).

POINTS TO PONDER

- Think about Morna Hooker's statement, 'His death is meaningless until God gives it meaning by raising him to life.'

- 'The cross of Jesus is both life-giving and death-dealing, and you can only share the life he gives if you will also die the death he dies.' Can you identify in your church and in yourself signs of his life but also things that still need to die?

- Now that you have finished the book, you might like to spend a little time recollecting anything in it that has been helpful to you and consider in practical and specific terms what your response should be.